MATHS

Book Two

Ray Allan
Henry Compton School, Fulham.

Martin Williams
Henry Compton School, Fulham.

Oxford University Press

Oxford University Press, Great Clarendon Street, Oxford OX2 6DP

Oxford   New York
Athens   Auckland   Bangkok   Bogota   Bombay
Buenos Aires   Calcutta   Cape Town   Dar es Salaam
Delhi   Florence   Hong Kong   Istanbul   Karachi
Kuala Lumpur   Madras   Madrid   Melbourne
Mexico City   Nairobi   Paris   Singapore
Taipei   Tokyo   Toronto

and associated companies in
Berlin Ibadan

Oxford is a trade mark of Oxford University Press

ISBN 0 19 834768 5

First published 1985
Reprinted 1987, 1988, 1990, 1991, 1992, 1993, 1994 (twice), 1995, 1996, 1997

The authors and the publisher are grateful to Guinness
Superlatives Ltd for information obtained on various world
records which are inserted in this book. Readers are invited
to consult the current edition of *The Guiness Book of Records*
for the latest information on these and other records.

Cover illustration by Terry Pastor
Text illustrations by Jon Riley

Artwork and Typesetting by BBG Ltd., Bristol
Printed in Italy by G. Canale & C. S.p.A. - Turin

Contents

1 **Fractions** *1*
Fair shares – shading fractions of shapes

2 **How much do you know?** *7*

3 **Time** *11*
Units – minutes – hours and minutes – days – the 24-hour clock

4 **The four rules 1** *18*
Addition – subtraction – multiplication – division

5 **Triangles and straight lines** *24*
Triangles – families of triangles – constructing triangles – angles in a triangle

6 **Using decimals** *31*
Measurement – using the decimal point – decimals less than one – decimals and money

7 **Codes** *39*

   Review 1 *42*

8 **Position** *44*
Giving directions – coordinates

9 **Distance** *51*
Units – measurements in metres

10 **Sorting into sets** *54*
Belonging to more than one set

   Review 2 *59*

11 **Graphs** *63*

12 **Time and distance** *66*
Travel graphs

13 **The four rules 2** *72*
Division and remainders – multiplying by 10

14 **Number patterns** *76*
Tables practice – factors – prime numbers – square numbers

   Review 3 *82*

15 **Street maths 1 – The Youth Club** *86*
Competitions – the canteen – fund raising – journeys

16 **Area** *91*

17 **Shape** *98*
Lines and circles – polygons – symmetry

18 **Algebra** *104*
Dealing with symbols – balancing problems

   Review 4 *110*

19 **Street maths 2 – Buying a bicycle** *116*
Sales and prices – nuts and bolts – journeys – competitions – puzzlers

Section 1 Fractions

Steve and Roger are sharing a cake.
Steve cuts it into two pieces.
But, as you can see the pieces are
not equal. . . . So:

Exercise 1

1. A cake has been shared three ways. Which drawing shows fair shares?

   a.    **b.**    **c.**

2. A block of ice cream is shared two ways. Which drawing shows fair shares?

   a.    **b.**    **c.**

3. A cake has been shared four ways. Which drawing shows fair shares?

   a.   **b.**   **c.**

4. A block of fudge is shared six ways. Which drawing shows fair shares?

   a.    **b.**    **c.**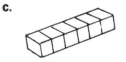

5. A stick of rock is shared five ways. Which drawing shows fair shares?

   a. 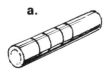   **b.** 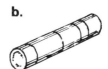   **c.**

Exercise 2

Here is a whole cake.

Four children are going to share it equally.

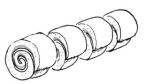

When the cake is cut into equal parts, each child gets one of the four parts.

Each child will get 'one part of 4' or $\frac{1}{4}$.

$\frac{1}{4}$ $\frac{1}{4}$ $\frac{1}{4}$ $\frac{1}{4}$

Express these amounts as fractions, like this.
One part of six is written as $\frac{1}{6}$.

1. One part of five is written as $\frac{*}{*}$

2. One part of seven is written as $\frac{*}{*}$

3. One part of six is written as $\frac{*}{*}$

4. One part of three is written as $\frac{*}{*}$

5. One part of two is written as $\frac{*}{*}$

6. One part of four is written as $\frac{*}{*}$

Exercise 3

Each child will get $\frac{1}{3}$ of the pie.

$\frac{1}{3}$ $\frac{1}{3}$ $\frac{1}{3}$

Here are three children.
They are going to share the pie equally.

Fill in the missing fractions in the table below.

number of children sharing pie	fraction of pie
3 children	$\frac{1}{3}$
5 children	$\frac{*}{*}$
9 children	$\frac{*}{*}$
8 children	$\frac{*}{*}$

number of children sharing pie	fraction of pie
2 children	$\frac{*}{*}$
6 children	$\frac{*}{*}$
4 children	$\frac{*}{*}$
10 children	$\frac{*}{*}$

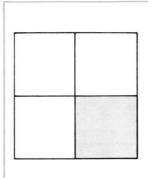

a. The shape is divided into 4 parts.

b. One part is coloured.

c. $\frac{1}{4}$ of the shape is coloured.

Exercise 4

Answer these three questions for each drawing below.

a. How many parts are there in each shape?

b. How many parts are coloured?

c. What fraction of the whole shape is coloured?

The first one is done for you.

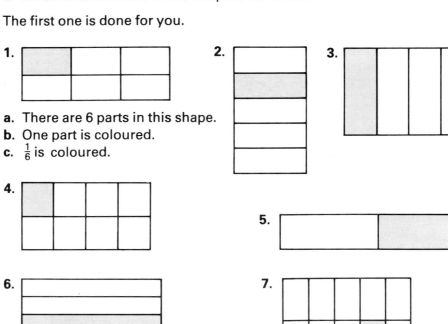

1.

a. There are 6 parts in this shape.
b. One part is coloured.
c. $\frac{1}{6}$ is coloured.

2.

3.

4.

5.

6.

7.

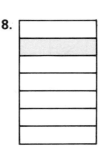

8.

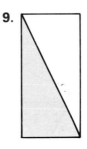

9.

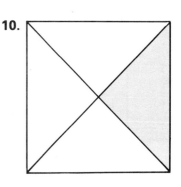

10.

Exercise 5

Match the coloured part of each shape to the correct fraction.
If you think shape 1 is $\frac{1}{2}$, you write **1 C**.

A	$\frac{1}{8}$
B	$\frac{1}{10}$
C	$\frac{1}{2}$
D	$\frac{1}{4}$
E	$\frac{1}{3}$

1.

2.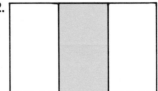

3.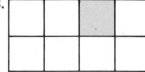

4.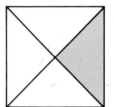

5.

Exercise 6

Match the coloured part of each shape to the correct fraction.

A	$\frac{1}{5}$
B	$\frac{1}{2}$
C	$\frac{1}{4}$
D	$\frac{1}{6}$
E	$\frac{1}{3}$

1. **2.**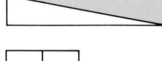

3.

4.

5.

Exercise 7

Match the coloured part of each shape to the correct fraction.

A	$\frac{1}{20}$
B	$\frac{1}{6}$
C	$\frac{1}{11}$
D	$\frac{1}{5}$
E	$\frac{1}{8}$
F	$\frac{1}{4}$
G	$\frac{1}{12}$
H	$\frac{1}{2}$
I	$\frac{1}{3}$
J	$\frac{1}{10}$

1. **2.**

3.

4.

5.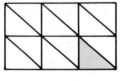

6.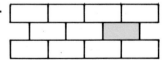

7.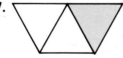

8.

9.

10.

a. The shape is divided into 3 parts.

b. Each part is a $\frac{1}{3}$ of the whole shape.

c. 2 parts are coloured so $\frac{2}{3}$ of the whole shape is coloured.

Exercise 8

Answer these three questions for each drawing.

a. How many parts are there in each shape?

b. What fraction is each part of the whole shape?

c. What fraction is coloured?

1.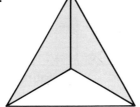

2.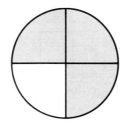

3.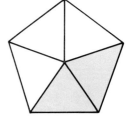

4.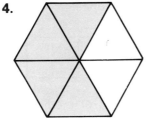

5.

6.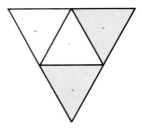

7.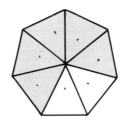

8.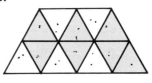

9.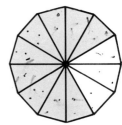

10.

11.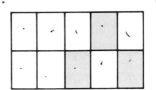

12.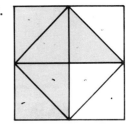

This shape is divided into 2 equal parts.
$\frac{1}{2}$ of the shape is coloured.

The same shape is now divided into 4 equal parts.
$\frac{2}{4}$ of the shape is coloured.

If you look carefully, you can see that $\frac{1}{2}$ of the shape is coloured.
So, $\frac{2}{4}$ is the same as $\frac{1}{2}$.

This shape is divided into 6 equal parts.
$\frac{3}{6}$ of the shape is coloured.

If you look carefully, you can see that $\frac{1}{2}$ of the shape is coloured.
So, $\frac{3}{6}$ is the same as $\frac{1}{2}$.

Exercise 9

1. Which of these drawings has exactly one half coloured?

a. $\frac{1}{6}$ coloured   b. $\frac{3}{6}$ coloured   c. $\frac{4}{9}$ coloured   d. $\frac{4}{8}$ coloured   e. $\frac{5}{10}$ coloured

2. These shapes have either $\frac{1}{2}$, $\frac{1}{3}$, $\frac{1}{4}$ or $\frac{1}{5}$ coloured.
   Copy and complete the sentences.

a. $\frac{3}{6}$ or $\frac{1}{*}$ coloured   b. $\frac{2}{8}$ or $\frac{1}{*}$ coloured   c. $\frac{3}{9}$ or $\frac{1}{*}$ coloured

d. $\frac{2}{10}$ or $\frac{1}{*}$ coloured   e. $\frac{4}{8}$ or $\frac{1}{*}$ coloured   f. $\frac{4}{12}$ or $\frac{1}{*}$ coloured

Exercise 10

Copy and complete these sentences.

1. $\frac{2}{4}$ is the same as $\frac{1}{*}$ 2. $\frac{3}{6}$ is the same as $\frac{1}{*}$ 3. $\frac{2}{6}$ is the same as $\frac{1}{*}$

4. $\frac{2}{10}$ is the same as $\frac{1}{*}$ 5. $\frac{3}{9}$ is the same as $\frac{1}{*}$ 6. $\frac{5}{10}$ is the same as $\frac{1}{*}$

7. $\frac{2}{8}$ is the same as $\frac{1}{*}$ 8. $\frac{4}{12}$ is the same as $\frac{1}{*}$ 9. $\frac{3}{12}$ is the same as $\frac{1}{*}$

10. $\frac{4}{8}$ is the same as $\frac{1}{*}$ 11. $\frac{6}{12}$ is the same as $\frac{1}{*}$ 12. $\frac{3}{15}$ is the same as $\frac{1}{*}$

A. Number work

1.	109 +238 ———	**2.**	398 +405 ———	**3.**	1206 +989 ———	**4.**	135 29 +258 ———
5.	87 −34 ———	**6.**	80 −27 ———	**7.**	415 −145 ———	**8.**	652 −147 ———
9.	5× 3 ———	**10.**	7× 4 ———	**11.**	2× 9 ———	**12.**	8× 3 ———
13.	2)‾1‾2‾	**14.**	5)‾2‾5‾	**15.**	4)‾2‾4‾	**16.**	6)‾3‾6‾

B. Perimeter

What is the length of the perimeter of each shape?
The drawings are not to scale.

1.
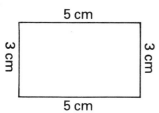

perimeter = _____ cm

2.
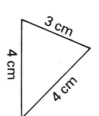

perimeter = _____ cm

3.
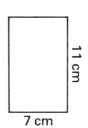

perimeter = _____ cm

4.
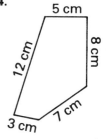

perimeter = _____ cm

C. Time

Match the two clocks which show the same time.
Clock 1 shows the same time as clock C, so you write 1C.

1.

2.

3.

4.

5.

A. 08 : 20

B. 11 : 45

C. 01 : 30

D. 01 : 55

E. 10 : 05

D. Sets   Group these into three set rings.

bread	shoe	hat	lorry	cake
sock	bus	chips	coat	car
chocolate	shirt	van	dress	taxi

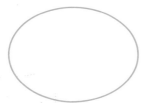   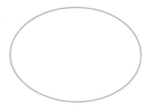   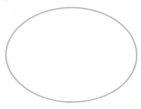

things to eat   things to wear   transport

E. Patterns in number Copy and complete these number patterns.

1. 10, 15, __ , 25, __   **2.** 5, 9, 13, 17, __, __

3. 6, 10, __, 18, __, 26   **4.** 2, 5, 8, 11, __, __,

5. 30, 27, 24, 21, __, __   **6.** 28, 25, 22, __, __, 13

7. 90, __, 70, 60, 50, __   **8.** 30, 25, 20, __, __, 5

F. Money

1.	**2.**	**3.**	**4.**	**5.**

£ : p	£ : p	£ : p	£ : p	£ : p
3 18	4 27	12 64	21 58	9 88
+ 5 21	+ 5 36	+34 94	+ 4 64	+37 27

Work out the cost of each lot of shopping.

 31p

 29p

 54p

 50p

6. How much would a tin of beans and a pack of butter cost?

7. How much would a bar of soap and a tin of beans cost?

8. How much would a tin of beans and a pack of cheese cost?

9. How much would a pack of cheese and a bar of soap cost?

10. How much would two tins of beans cost?

11. How much would two bars of soap cost?

G. Angles

What angles are shown on these protractors?

1.

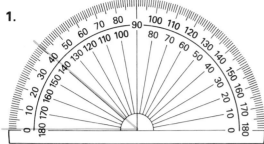

2.

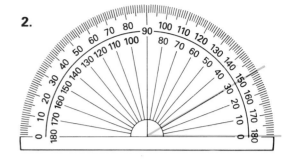

3.

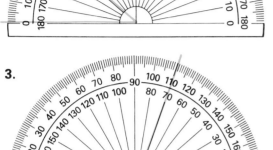

4.

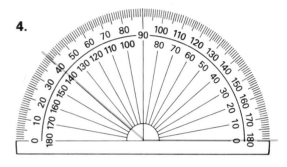

H. Problems

1. Tom has 56p, Gill has 30p and Tim has 40p. How much have they in total?

2. If there are 11 sweets in a packet, how many sweets are in 3 packets?

3. There are 32 people in a room. If 6 people leave, how many are left?

4. Two children share 18p equally. How much does each get?

5. What is the total of £5, £4, £7 and 26p?

6. Mary has 97p. She spends 57p. How much has she left?

7. What is six times three?

8. How many times does 3 go into 15?

9. Add four to ninety-nine.

10. Take 222 from 555.

I. Algebra

Write down the missing numbers.

1. $* + 5 = 11$ **2.** $* + 12 = 20$ **3.** $9 + * = 21$ **4.** $12 - * = 10$

5. $* - 3 = 2$

w is worth 4 x is worth 7
y is worth 2 z is worth 3
So what is the value of these expressions?

6. $x + z = *$ **7.** $z + y = *$ **8.** $x + y = *$ **9.** $w + x - z = *$

10. $x + z + w - y = *$

J. Statistics

What numbers are shown on these tallies?

1. ⊺⊦⊦ ⊺⊦⊦ II = ∗   2. ⊺⊦⊦ ⊺⊦⊦ ⊺⊦⊦ III = ∗

3. ⊺⊦⊦ ⊺⊦⊦ ⊺⊦⊦ ⊺⊦⊦ III = ∗   4. ⊺⊦⊦ ⊺⊦⊦ ⊺⊦⊦ ⊺⊦⊦ ⊺⊦⊦ ⊺⊦⊦ = ∗

5. ⊺⊦⊦ ⊺⊦⊦ ⊺⊦⊦ ⊺⊦⊦ ⊺⊦⊦ ⊺⊦⊦ ⊺⊦⊦ ⊺⊦⊦ ⊺⊦⊦ I = ∗

This bar chart shows the attendance of six classes in one day.
Answer the questions about the bar chart.

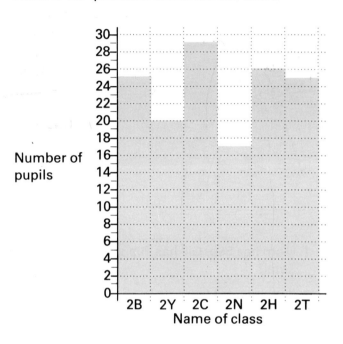

6. Which class had the highest attendance?   7. Which class had the lowest attendance?

8. How many pupils in 2Y attended?   9. How many pupils in 2H attended?

10. How many pupils in 2B attended?   11. How many pupils in 2N attended?

12. How many pupils in 2C attended?   13. How many pupils in 2T attended?

14. Which classes had the same attendance?   15. Which class had 29 pupils attending?

K. Shapes

1. Copy and complete these symmetrical letters to make a word.

Draw the completed symmetrical shapes below.

2.   3.   4.   5.   6.

Section 3   **Time**

Seconds – minutes hours – days – months years

These are some of the units of time. It is necessary to choose useful units for measuring time.

Here are some crazy records.
Note the different units used for each record.

The world record for eating 91 pickled onions is 68 seconds.

M. Lotito ate a bicycle in 15 days.

Mr. Anadan balanced on one leg for 33 hours.

Jay Gwaltney ate a tree trunk 3·35 m long in 3 days 17 hours.

The world's oldest living tree is over 6000 years

Exercise 1

Which unit would you use to measure these lengths of time?

1. The amount of time you sleep each night.

2. The time taken to tie your shoe laces.

3. The time taken to write your name once.

4. The time taken to travel to school.

5. The amount of time until next Sunday.

6. The time taken to eat a bag of crisps.

7. The time taken to clap your hands 15 times.

8. The time taken to brush your teeth.

Clocks and calendars are used to record or to measure time.

Exercise 2

Copy and complete these sentences.

1. There are ___ minutes in an hour.

2. There are ___ days in a week.

3. There are ___ months in a year.

4. There are ___ seconds in a minute.

5. An hour is (longer/shorter) than a minute.

6. A month is (longer/shorter) than a year.

7. A minute is (longer/shorter) than a second.

8. A month is (longer/shorter) than a week.

Minutes

Exercise 3

1. Rupert took part in a car rally.
   Clock A shows the time when he started.
   Clock B shows the time when he finished.
   How many minutes did he take?

Clock A   Clock B

2. Miranda went to her science lesson.
   Clock A shows when the lesson began.
   Clock B shows when the lesson finished.
   How many minutes have passed?

Clock A   Clock B

How many minutes have passed between the times shown?

3. **4.** **5.**

6. **7.** **8.**

Exercise 4

1. Tom left for school at 8 o'clock. He arrived at 20 minutes past 8.
   How long did it take him?

2. Mary started her exercises at '10 past 4' and finished at '25 past 4'.
   How long was she doing her exercises?

3. Mum started making tea at '10 to 4' and finished at '15 minutes past 4'.
   How long did it take her to make tea?

4. Dad started washing the windows at 3 o'clock and finished at '10 to 4'.
   How long did it take him to wash the windows?

5. A television programme started at '5 past 6' and finished at '5 to 7'.
   How long did the programme last?

This clock says '30 minutes past 4', or 'half-past 4'.

 This clock says 'a quarter to 4'.

 This clock says 'a quarter past 4'.

Exercise 5

Copy and complete these sentences.

1. This clock shows a quarter past 6. This is the same as ____ minutes past 6.

2. This clock shows a quarter to 4. This is the same as ____ minutes to 4.

3. This clock shows half-past 10. This is the same as ____ minutes past 10.

4. This clock shows 2.45. This is the same as a quarter to ____ .

5. This clock shows 6.45. This is the same as ____ minutes to 7.

Exercise 6

Write down how many minutes pass between

half past

quarter to — quarter past

1. 6 o'clock and half-past 6

2. 9 o'clock and a quarter-past 9

3. 2 o'clock and a quarter to 3

4. half-past 9 and 10 o'clock

5. a quarter to 7 and 7 o'clock

6. a quarter to 5 and a quarter-past 5

7. half-past 6 and 7 o'clock

8. a quarter to 10 and a quarter-past 10

9. a quarter-past 2 and a quarter to 3

10. half-past 8 and a quarter to 9

Hours and minutes

Exercise 7

1. Cathy left for work at 7 o'clock.
   She got to work at 20 minutes past 8.
   How many hours and minutes did her
   journey take?

2. Robert starts playing football at 3 o'clock.
   He finishes at half-past 4.
   How many hours and minutes does the
   game last?

3. Mary drove to her friend's house in York.
   She left at 8 o'clock and arrived at
   half-past 9. How many hours and minutes
   did the journey take?

Exercise 8

Mick took part in a marathon. During the race, he saw a number of clocks.
The race started at 2 o'clock.
How long had he been running when he saw

1. The Town Hall clock?   2. The clock in the square?

3. The Station clock?   4. The Market clock?   5. The clock at the finish?

Days

To record days, weeks and
months, we use a calendar.

Here is a calendar showing
the month of October.

Look at the calendar, then
answer the questions below.

October					
Sunday		6	13	20	27
Monday		7	14	21	28
Tuesday	1	8	15	22	29
Wednesday	2	9	16	23	30
Thursday	3	10	17	24	31
Friday	4	11	18	25	
Saturday	5	12	19	26	

1. How many days are there in October?

2. On which day does October begin?

3. On which day will 23rd October fall?

4. What date will it be on the last Tuesday of the month?

5. On which day does October end?

6. What will be the date on the first Thursday of the month?

7. On which day will 16th October fall?

8. On which day will 8th October fall?

9. What is the date marked with a X ?

10. What is the date marked with a √ ?

Use the calendar above to answer these questions.

1. Tom begins his holiday on Thursday 10th October. The last day of his
   holiday is Sunday 20th October. How long is the holiday?

2. The first day of Anne's school journey is marked with a √ and the
   last day with a X . How many days does the journey last?

3. Jenny's exams begin on Monday 21st October and end on Thursday
   24th October. How many days do the exams last?

4. Bob's holiday begins on Monday 14th October. He has 9 days holiday.
   What is the date of the last day of his holiday?

5. Mandy's holiday begins on Wednesday 2nd October. She has 14 days
   holiday. What is the date of the last day of her holiday?

6. a. How many Sundays are there in this month?
   b. How many Tuesdays are there in this month?
   c. How many Fridays are there in this month?

The 24-hour clock

Captain Bulldog wants to see his soldiers at 7 o'clock, but the soldiers are confused. Does he mean 7 o'clock in the morning or 7 o'clock at night?

To clear up the confusion, the captain repeats the order using the 24-hour clock.

He says he wants to see the soldiers at 19.00 hours. What does this mean?

We say a day begins a moment after 12 o'clock midnight, and lasts for the next 24 hours. The hour hand of a clock travels around the clock face twice a day. So 7 o'clock will appear twice in a day.

Using the 24-hour clock, a day still starts at 12 midnight.
After 12 noon, we do not go back to 1 o'clock or 1 p.m.
We carry on, 12.00, 13.00, and so on to 23.59.

Exercise 11

Using this time diagram, copy and complete the sentences below.

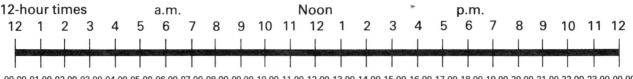

1. 6 a.m. is the same as____
2. 9 a.m. is the same as____
3. 4 a.m. is the same as____
4. 2 a.m. is the same as____
5. 2 p.m. is the same as____
6. 6 p.m. is the same as____
7. 10 p.m. is the same as____
8. 4 p.m. is the same as____
9. 08.00 is the same as____a.m.
10. 10.00 is the same as____a.m.
11. 14.00 is the same as____p.m.
12. 21.00 is the same as____p.m.
13. 06.00 is the same as____
14. 15.00 is the same as____
15. 23.00 is the same as____

a.m.  p.m.

The time is 8.30 in the morning (8.30 a.m.).

A 24-hour clock would show 08.30.

The time is 2.15 in the afternoon (2.15 p.m).

A 24-hour clock would show 14.15.

With the 24-hour clock, we do not use a.m. or p.m.

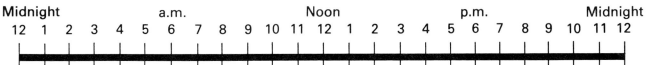

24-hour clock

Exercise 12

Write the time shown on each clock in the 24-hour system.

1. a.m.
2. a.m.
3. a.m.
4. p.m.

5. p.m.
6. a.m.
7. p.m.
8. p.m.

9. p.m.
10. p.m.
11. a.m.
12. p.m.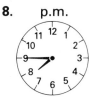

Exercise 13

Write these 24-hour times as 12-hour times. Remember to put in whether the time is a.m. or p.m.

1. 05.30   **2.** 07.15   **3.** 13.30

4. 18.00   **5.** 09.20   **6.** 16.45

7. 04.20   **8.** 11.25   **9.** 19.30

10. 22.10   **11.** 10.10   **12.** 23.50

Section 4   The four rules 1

Addition

Addition workcard 1

1.	23 +14	**2.**	46 +23	**3.**	22 +57
4.	36 +10	**5.**	54 +20	**6.**	20 +47
7.	26 +16	**8.**	37 +36	**9.**	45 +27
10.	38 +35	**11.**	44 +28	**12.**	67 +18

Addition workcard 2

1.	56 +19	**2.**	24 +28	**3.**	36 +26
4.	48 +28	**5.**	19 +37	**6.**	57 +28
7.	36 +39	**8.**	43 +48	**9.**	57 +37
10.	66 +18	**11.**	49 +29	**12.**	18 +57

Addition workcard 3

1.	18 +12	**2.**	35 +25	**3.**	41 +19
4.	54 +36	**5.**	27 +23	**6.**	16 +24
7.	25 +29	**8.**	46 +47	**9.**	38 +32
10.	16 +49	**11.**	58 +18	**12.**	37 +33

Addition workcard 4

1.	126 +253	**2.**	214 +375	**3.**	443 +456
4.	256 +116	**5.**	347 +224	**6.**	559 +315
7.	260 +153	**8.**	167 +190	**9.**	371 +154
10.	256 +250	**11.**	273 +133	**12.**	519 +190

Addition workcard 5

1.	41 +80	**2.**	78 +46	**3.**	86 +66
4.	53 +63	**5.**	86 +91	**6.**	98 +70
7.	77 +43	**8.**	55 +55	**9.**	79 +158
10.	189 +36	**11.**	160 +63	**12.**	99 +131

Addition workcard 6

1.	186 +144	**2.**	263 +167	**3.**	485 +236
4.	588 +144	**5.**	158 +354	**6.**	627 +297
7.	199 +401	**8.**	428 +272	**9.**	349 +155
10.	277 +273	**11.**	178 +225	**12.**	405 +398

1. 140 37 +121	**2.** 61 105 +33	**3.** 100 23 +9
4. 28 132 +7	**5.** 66 118 +15	**6.** 212 8 +37
7. 250 128 +19	**8.** 34 106 +120	**9.** 411 9 +154
10. 116 118 +42	**11.** 306 62 +160	**12.** 227 10 +181

1. 133 153 +81	**2.** 225 281 +50	**3.** 40 67 +191
4. 292 144 +61	**5.** 350 43 +175	**6.** 171 271 +180
7. 167 43 +322	**8.** 245 368 +61	**9.** 459 63 +184
10. 249 27 +26	**11.** 38 208 +49	**12.** 167 188 +68

Exercise 1   Copy and complete these sentences.

1. 625 There is a __ in the 100's column.
2. 252 There is a __ in the 10's column.
3. 2518 There is a __ in the 100's column.
4. 4105 There is a __ in the 1000's column.
5. 2353 There is a __ in the 1's column.
6. 6225 There is a __ in the 1000's column.
7. 3027 There is a __ in the 1000's column.
8. 5352 There is a __ in the 1000's column.

1. 355 +1410	**2.** 2236 +522	**3.** 547 +1142
4. 606 +1752	**5.** 726 +2423	**6.** 1525 +862
7. 2918 +528	**8.** 1539 +623	**9.** 856 +816
10. 764 +592	**11.** 788 +450	**12.** 692 +828

1. 4288 +2243	**2.** 2357 +5257	**3.** 1884 +3057
4. 2852 +1398	**5.** 2582 +2639	**6.** 1958 +2074
7. 2535 +3595	**8.** 6816 +1886	**9.** 3658 +2642
10. 5886 +2819	**11.** 1943 +2057	**12.** 5174 +1826

Subtraction

Subtraction workcard 1

1. 428 −213	**2.** 649 −125	**3.** 844 −123
4. 388 −256	**5.** 573 −113	**6.** 285 −182
7. 560 −116	**8.** 453 −125	**9.** 891 −228
10. 650 −325	**11.** 770 −218	**12.** 964 −229

Subtraction workcard 2

1. 908 −225	**2.** 806 −354	**3.** 526 −175
4. 818 −277	**5.** 425 −261	**6.** 607 −150
7. 546 −266	**8.** 817 −280	**9.** 335 −175
10. 918 −320	**11.** 756 −296	**12.** 460 −180

Subtraction workcard 3

1. 470 −216	**2.** 852 −182	**3.** 782 −206
4. 380 −176	**5.** 650 −207	**6.** 473 −165
7. 793 −487	**8.** 540 −138	**9.** 614 −207
10. 532 −282	**11.** 605 −360	**12.** 456 −176

Subtraction workcard 4

1. 690 −308	**2.** 580 −525	**3.** 873 −805
4. 571 −508	**5.** 948 −73	**6.** 603 −91
7. 238 −78	**8.** 417 −70	**9.** 539 −59
10. 845 −157	**11.** 535 −269	**12.** 623 −67

Exercise 2

1. There are 23 people on a bus and 17 get off. How many are left?

2. A match box holds 40 matches, and 23 are taken. How many are left?

3. There are 32 sweets in a box. If 15 are eaten, how many are left?

4. There are 41 pupils in a room. If 9 pupils leave, how many are left?

5. A lorry contains 100 boxes. If 43 are unloaded, how many are left?

6. Clare has 65p. She spends 18p. How much has she left?

7. A shop-keeper has 125 apples. He sells 19 apples. How many has he left?

8. Mary has 74 buttons in a tin. She takes out 9. How many are left?

9. There are 52 cards in a pack. If you removed 21, how many are left?

10. Roger has 107 comics. He gives 38 away. How many has he left?

Subtraction workcard 5

1. 250 −116	**2.** 505 −125	**3.** 960 −239
4. 607 −436	**5.** 405 −115	**6.** 500 −270
7. 403 −153	**8.** 560 −159	**9.** 304 −124
10. 300 −160	**11.** 430 −125	**12.** 370 −264

Subtraction workcard 6

1. 334 −250	**2.** 625 −565	**3.** 702 −642
4. 210 −170	**5.** 436 −380	**6.** 543 −463
7. 830 −165	**8.** 730 −343	**9.** 550 −266
10. 622 −285	**11.** 432 −235	**12.** 513 −148

Subtraction workcard 7

1. 3525 −2415	**2.** 6505 −1400	**3.** 3660 −2360
4. 2542 −1416	**5.** 6850 −4536	**6.** 9633 −6017
7. 8836 −5163	**8.** 6915 −2565	**9.** 4704 −2340
10. 6732 −1156	**11.** 3940 −1056	**12.** 6611 −3235

Subtraction workcard 8

1. 6523 −166	**2.** 3582 −576	**3.** 4220 −600
4. 5413 −2413	**5.** 3232 −1232	**6.** 2583 −503
7. 6631 −4714	**8.** 5280 −1715	**9.** 4050 −2316
10. 5342 −2565	**11.** 3320 −659	**12.** 2123 −578

Exercise 3

1. Take one from 100.
2. Take 90 from 100.
3. Take 5 from 50.
4. Take one from 200.
5. Take 10 from 100.
6. Take 10 from 300.
7. Take 100 from 1000.
8. Take 50 from 600.
9. Take 5 from 200.
10. Take 55 from 500.

Multiplication

Exercise 4   Copy and complete these statements. Question 1 is done for you.

1. 4 lots of 2 = 8
2. 3 lots of 3 = *
3. 5 lots of 2 = *
4. 4 lots of 3 = *
5. 4 lots of 4 = *
6. 6 lots of 2 = *
7. 3 lots of 5 = *
8. 2 lots of 7 = *
9. 2 lots of 8 = *
10. 5 lots of 4 = *
11. $2 \times 5 = *$
12. $3 \times 4 = *$
13. $6 \times 3 = *$
14. $4 \times 3 = *$
15. $2 \times 6 = *$
16. $7 \times 3 = *$
17. $5 \times 5 = *$
18. $6 \times 5 = *$
19. $2 \times 10 = *$
20. $5 \times 10 = *$

Multiplication workcard 1

1. 12 ×
   3
2. 14 ×
   2
3. 21 ×
   4
4. 13 ×
   3
5. 23 ×
   3
6. 31 ×
   2
7. 41 ×
   2
8. 24 ×
   2
9. 32 ×
   2
10. 20 ×
    3
11. 22 ×
    3
12. 23 ×
    3

Multiplication workcard 2

1. 5 ×
   3
2. 8 ×
   2
3. 6 ×
   3
4. 9 ×
   2
5. 5 ×
   4
6. 6 ×
   5
7. 15 ×
   3
8. 14 ×
   4
9. 16 ×
   3
10. 13 ×
    4
11. 17 ×
    2
12. 13 ×
    5

Multiplication workcard 3

1. 23 ×
   4
2. 16 ×
   5
3. 24 ×
   4
4. 25 ×
   3
5. 15 ×
   5
6. 26 ×
   3
7. 27 ×
   2
8. 15 ×
   6
9. 18 ×
   3
10. 16 ×
    6
11. 29 ×
    2
12. 28 ×
    3

Multiplication workcard 4

1. 213 ×
   2
2. 142 ×
   2
3. 232 ×
   3
4. 143 ×
   2
5. 212 ×
   3
6. 312 ×
   3
7. 125 ×
   3
8. 214 ×
   4
9. 116 ×
   2
10. 216 ×
    3
11. 127 ×
    2
12. 215 ×
    4

Exercise 5

1. What is 3 times 10?
2. What is 5 multiplied by 6?
3. What is 12 times 2?
4. What do 4 lots of 6 make?
5. What do 7 lots of 4 make?
6. What is 9 multiplied by 3?
7. What do 8 groups of 4 make?
8. What is 4 multiplied by 11?
9. What is 10 times 5?
10. What do 7 lots of 5 make?
11. What do 12 groups of 3 make?
12. What is 2 times 16?

Division

Exercise 6

1. Share 10 sweets into 2 groups.

 $10 \div 2 = *$

2. Share 12 cakes into 3 groups.

 $12 \div 3 = *$

3. Share 16 pence into 2 groups.

 $16 \div 2 = *$

4. Share 15 apples into 3 groups.

 $15 \div 3 = *$

5. Share 24 pencils into 4 groups.

 $24 \div 4 = *$

6. Share 21 pies into 3 groups.

$21 \div 3 = *$

Division workcard 1

1. $12 \div 4 =$	**2.** $14 \div 2 =$	**3.** $16 \div 2 =$
4. $10 \div 2 =$	**5.** $18 \div 2 =$	**6.** $20 \div 5 =$
7. $12 \div 3 =$	**8.** $16 \div 4 =$	**9.** $24 \div 6 =$
10. $24 \div 4 =$	**11.** $21 \div 3 =$	**12.** $30 \div 3 =$

Division workcard 2

1. $21 \div 7 =$	**2.** $40 \div 5 =$	**3.** $20 \div 2 =$
4. $24 \div 3 =$	**5.** $18 \div 3 =$	**6.** $25 \div 5 =$
7. $27 \div 9 =$	**8.** $24 \div 8 =$	**9.** $30 \div 6 =$
10. $18 \div 9 =$	**11.** $28 \div 4 =$	**12.** $35 \div 5 =$

Exercise 7

1. If 3 people share 18 books, how many do they each get?

 $3\overline{)18}$

2. If 5 people share 15 cakes, how many do they each get?

 $5\overline{)15}$

3. If 4 children share 16 comics, how many do they each get?

 $4\overline{)16}$

4. If 6 children share 18 marbles, how many do they each get?

$6\overline{)18}$

5. 3 children share 24 sweets. How many do they each get?

 $3\overline{)24}$

6. 4 children share 20p. How much do they each get?

 $4\overline{)20}$

Division workcard 3

1. $2\overline{)8}$	**2.** $2\overline{)12}$	**3.** $3\overline{)9}$
4. $2\overline{)16}$	**5.** $4\overline{)8}$	**6.** $3\overline{)6}$
7. $3\overline{)12}$	**8.** $2\overline{)18}$	**9.** $4\overline{)12}$
10. $5\overline{)25}$	**11.** $4\overline{)16}$	**12.** $5\overline{)15}$

Division workcard 4

1. $2\overline{)10}$	**2.** $3\overline{)15}$	**3.** $2\overline{)20}$
4. $3\overline{)18}$	**5.** $4\overline{)20}$	**6.** $4\overline{)28}$
7. $5\overline{)20}$	**8.** $3\overline{)30}$	**9.** $6\overline{)12}$
10. $5\overline{)30}$	**11.** $6\overline{)18}$	**12.** $6\overline{)24}$

Triangles and straight lines

Triangles

Exercise 1

Look at the shapes below, and decide which of them are triangles.

1.   2.  3.   4.

5. 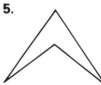 6.   7.   8.

9. 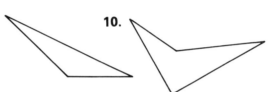 10. 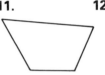 11.   12.

Exercise 2

Look carefully at the shapes below and say how many triangles you can see in each drawing.

1.  2.   3.   4.

5.   6. 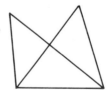 7.

8. 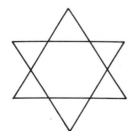 9. 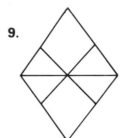 10.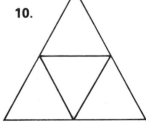

Families of triangles

There are three families of triangles: scalene triangles
isosceles triangles
and equilateral triangles

Scalene triangle

The length of each side is different.

The size of each angle is also different.

Isosceles triangle

The length of two sides is the same.

The size of two angles is also the same.

Equilateral triangle

All three sides are of the same length.

All three angles are also equal.

Exercise 3

Measure each triangle and write down the family to which you think it belongs.

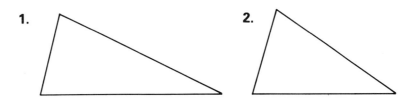

1.

2.

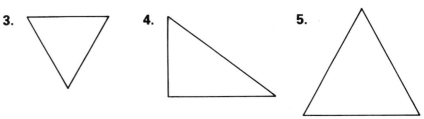

3.

4.

5.

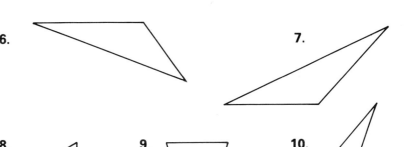

6.

7.

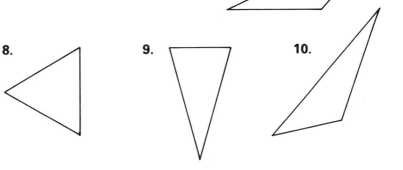

8.

9.

10.

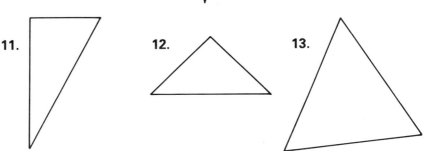

11.

12.

13.

Constructing triangles

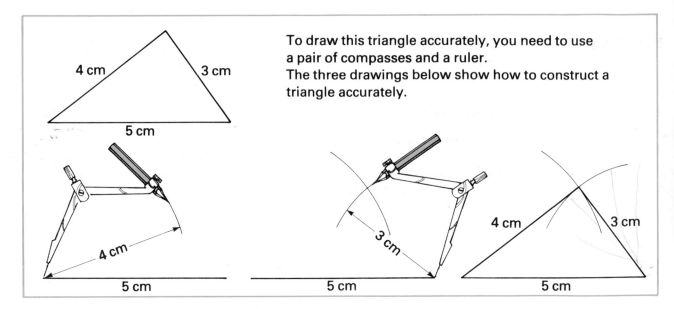

To draw this triangle accurately, you need to use a pair of compasses and a ruler.
The three drawings below show how to construct a triangle accurately.

Exercise 4

Use a ruler and compasses to construct the triangles below.
The drawings are not drawn to scale.

1.
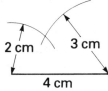
4 cm   3 cm
5 cm

2.
4 cm   4 cm
6 cm

3.
2 cm   3 cm
4 cm

4.
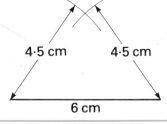
4·5 cm   4·5 cm
6 cm

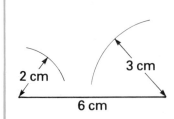
2 cm   3 cm
6 cm

This drawing cannot be finished because the two arcs will never cross.

For a triangle to be drawn, any one pair of sides must always add up to a distance longer than the third side.

Exercise 5

Say which sets of measurements below would not form triangles if they were drawn.

1. 2 cm, 4 cm, 5 cm.

2. 5 cm, 2 cm, 1 cm.

3. 9 cm, 4 cm, 6 cm.

4. 10 cm, 5 cm, 5 cm.

5. 15 cm, 7 cm, 6 cm.

6. 4 cm, 11 cm, 8 cm.

Exercise 6

Use a protractor to measure the
angles of these two triangles.
Copy and complete the sentences below.

1. Angle a = _____ °

2. Angle b = _____ °

3. Angle c = _____ °

4. The three angles of the triangle add up to _____ °

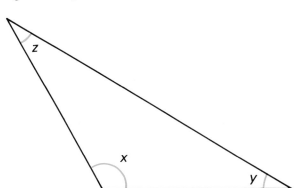

5. Angle x = _____ °

6. Angle y = _____ °

7. Angle z = _____ °

8. The three angles of the
   triangle add up to _____ °

If you have measured the angles carefully and added accurately, you
should have found that the three angles of each triangle add up to 180°.

Remember: the angles of a triangle add up to 180°.

Exercise 7

Here is a page from Martin's Maths book. He has drawn some triangles
and measured their angles, but he has not measured carefully. Make a list
of the triangles whose angles have been measured wrongly.

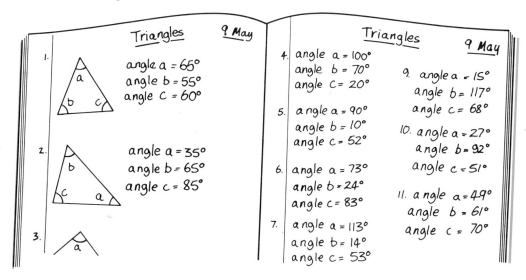

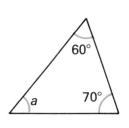

In the last exercise we found that the angles of a triangle add up to 180°.

If you know two of the angles, you can find the third angle.

angle a + 60° + 70° = 180°
So, angle a = 50°

Exercise 8

Work out the size of the angles marked with a letter.
Do not measure the angles.

1.

2.

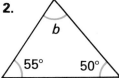

3.

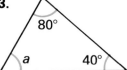

4.

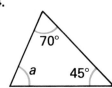

5.

6.

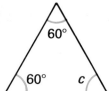

7.

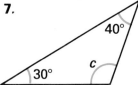

8.

9.

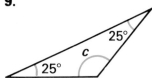

10.

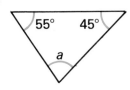

11.

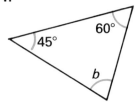

12.

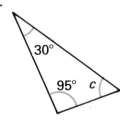

13.

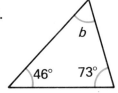

14.

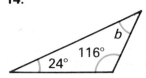

15.

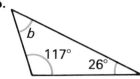

Angles in a triangle

The angles in a triangle
and
angles on a straight line
=

180°

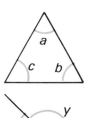

$a + b + c = 180°$

$x + y = 180°$

To show that angles in a triangle equal a straight angle (180°)

Cut a triangle out of card,
and mark the three angles
with stars.

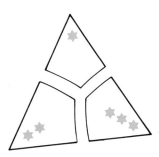

Cut the three angles
from the triangle.

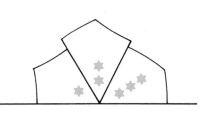

Bring the three angles together
on a straight line. The angles
will add up to a straight angle
or 180°.

Exercise 9

Re-draw these diagrams and calculate the angles marked with letters in each question.

1.

2.

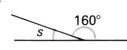

3.

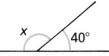

4.

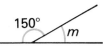

5.

6.

7.

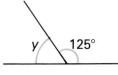

8.

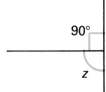

9.

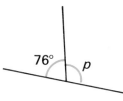

10.

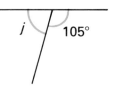

11.

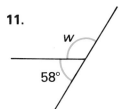

12.

To find both of the unknown angles you must use
two facts: a straight angle = 180°
             angles in a triangle =180°

angle *a* = 70°
so angle *b* = 50°

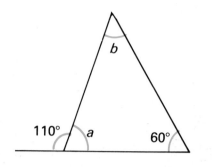

Exercise 10

Re-draw these diagrams and calculate the angles marked with letters.

1.

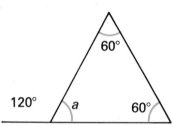

2.

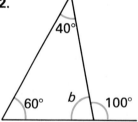

3.

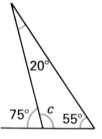

4.

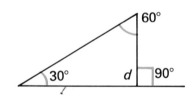

5.

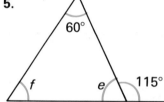

6.

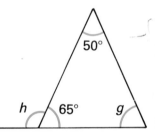

Exercise 11

Re-draw these diagrams and calculate the three lettered angles in each
question.

1.

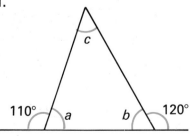

2.

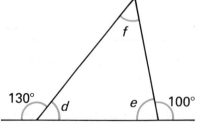

3.

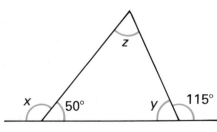

Using decimals

The children here are finding out about plants, animals, feathers and other objects.

The children measure the items in their collection.

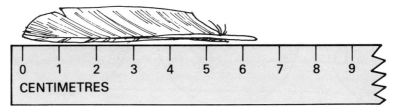

This feather is just over 6 cm long.

To measure more accurately, the children used this type of ruler.

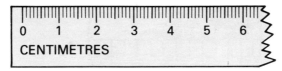

Each centimetre is divided into 10 equal parts. So each part is one-tenth ($\frac{1}{10}$) of a centimetre

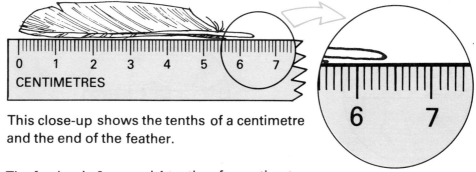

This close-up shows the tenths of a centimetre and the end of the feather.

The feather is 6 cm and 4 tenths of a centimetre.

Exercise 1

This is a table of measurements made by the children.

	Item	cm	tenths of cm
1.	Worm	5	9
2.	Oak leaf		
3.	Beetle		
4.	Feather		
5.	Earwig		
6.	Butterfly		
7.	Bluebell Stem		
8.	Tadpole		
9.	Holly Leaf		
10.	Ear of wheat		

Copy the table and fill in the measurements for each close-up.

1. Worm

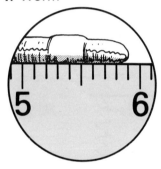

2. Oak leaf

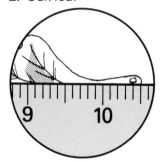

3. Beetle

4. Feather

5. Earwig

6. Butterfly

7. Bluebell stem

8. Tadpole

9. Holly leaf

10. Ear of wheat

Using the decimal point

The feather is 6 cm and 4 tenths of a cm long.

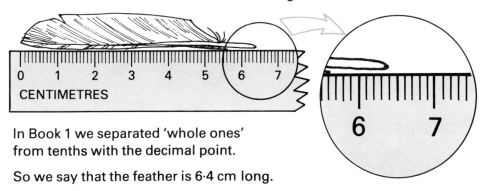

In Book 1 we separated 'whole ones' from tenths with the decimal point.

So we say that the feather is 6·4 cm long.

Exercise 2 Re-draw the table in Exercise 1. This time use the decimal point in the table,

Like this:

	Item	Length in cm
1.	worm	5·9 cm
2.	Oak leaf	10·5 cm

Exercise 3 Copy and complete the table below.

1.	6 cm and 4 tenths	6·4 cm
2.	2 cm and 1 tenth	*
3.	5 cm and 0 tenths	5.0 cm
4.	4 cm and 7 tenths	*
5.	3 cm and 9 tenths	*
6.	8 cm and 8 tenths	*
7.	1 cm and 3 tenths	*
8.	13 cm and 2 tenths	13·2 cm
9.	7 cm and 0 tenths	*
10.	15 cm and 0 tenths	*
11.	11 cm and 9 tenths	*
12.	54 cm and 3 tenths	*
13.	16 cm and 0 tenths	*
14.	43 cm and 5 tenths	*
15.	16 cm and 6 tenths	*
16.	27 cm and 4 tenths	*
17.	15 cm and 2 tenths	*
18.	70 cm and 0 tenths	*
19.	61 cm and 8 tenths	*
20.	39 cm and 2 tenths	*

Exercise 4

Measure these objects to the nearest tenth of a centimetre. Make a table like that in Exercise 2.

a. Earthworm

b. Stickleback fish

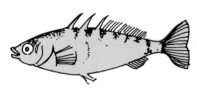

c. Ear of wheat

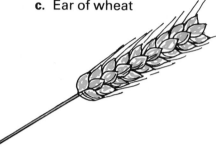

d. Oak leaf

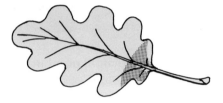

e. Beetle

f. Snail

g. Holly leaf

h. Caterpillar

i. Newt

Exercise 5

Answer these questions about the objects above.

1. Which drawing is exactly 3·0 cm long?

2. Which drawing is 5·6 cm long?

3. Which drawing is 4·9 cm long?

4. Which drawing is 3·2 cm long?

5. Which drawing is the longer, the holly leaf or the ear of wheat?

6. Which drawing is nearly 5 cm long?

7. Which is longer, the beetle or the caterpillar?

8. Which is the longest drawing?

9. Which is the shortest drawing?

10. Which drawings are longer than 7 cm?

Decimals less than one

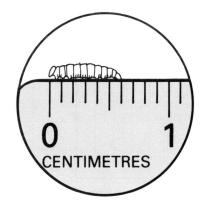

The children find some bugs.

The length of the bug in this close-up is less than one whole centimetre.

It is 6 tenths of a centimetre long.

This is written as 0·6 cm and we say it is 'nought-point-six centimetres' long.

This means 'no whole centimetres and six tenths of a centimetre'.

Exercise 6

Copy and complete this table giving the length of the bugs.

Bug number	Length
1	
2	
3	
4	
5	
6	
7	
8	

1.

2.

3.

4.

5.

6.

7.

8.

a.

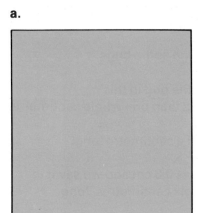

This square is
one whole unit or 1.0

b.

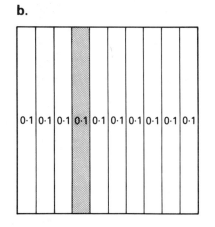

The whole unit has been divided
into ten equal strips.
Each strip is a tenth or 0·1.

c.

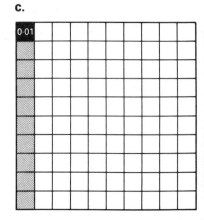

The whole unit has been
divided into one hundred
equal squares. Each square
is a hundredth or 0·01.

Exercise 7

1. Look at diagrams **a.** and **b.** Which is larger, 0·1 or 1·0?

2. Look at diagram **b.** How many parts of 0·1 make the whole unit?

3. Look at diagram **c.** How many 0·01 parts make the whole unit?

4. Look at diagrams **b.** and **c.** Which is the larger part, 0·1 or 0·01?

5. Look at diagrams **b.** and **c.** How many 0·01 parts make 0·1?

Exercise 8

Write down the numbers shown in each drawing.
Use the drawings on the left for help. The first one is done for you.

1 unit

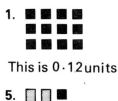

This is 0·12 units

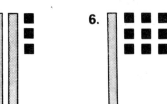

0·1 unit

5.

6.

7.

8.

9.

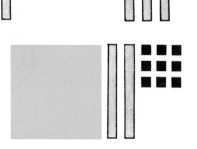

10.

■ 0·01 units.

Here is the square again representing one whole unit.
It has been divided into 100 equal squares.

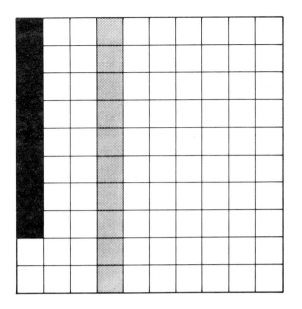

The part shaded in black represents eight hundredths.
This may be written

$\frac{8}{100}$ or 0·08

The part shaded in grey is ten hundredths.
This is the same as one tenth, so it
is written

$\frac{10}{100}$ or $\frac{1}{10}$

0·10 or 0·1

Exercise 9   Copy and complete the table below.

	Fraction	Decimal
5 hundredths	$\frac{5}{100}$	0·05
2 hundredths	$\frac{2}{100}$	*
* hundredths	$\frac{7}{100}$	*
3 hundredths	*	*
19 hundredths	*	0·19
52 hundredths	*	*
* hundredths	*	0·75
87 hundredths	*	*
* hundredths	$\frac{94}{100}$	*
1 whole and 3 hundredths	$1\frac{3}{100}$	1·03
2 wholes and 4 hundredths	*	*
6 wholes and 9 hundredths	*	*
3 wholes and 7 hundredths	*	*
* wholes and * hundredths	$5\frac{21}{100}$	*
* wholes and * hundredths	*	7.50

One pound is the same as ten 10p pieces.

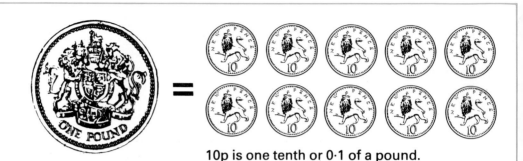

10p is one tenth or 0·1 of a pound.

Exercise 10

Copy and complete these sentences. The first one has been done for you.

1. 90p is the same as £0·90

2. 30p is the same as £0·**

3. 60p is the same as £0·**

4. 20p is the same as £0·**

5. 80p is the same as £0·**

6. 50p is the same as £0·**

7. ** p is the same as £0·70

8. ** p is the same as £0·40

9. ** p is the same as £0·10

10. ** p is the same as £0·30

One pound is the same as one hundred 1p pieces.

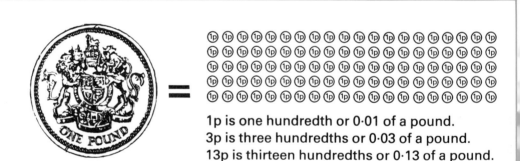

1p is one hundredth or 0·01 of a pound.
3p is three hundredths or 0·03 of a pound.
13p is thirteen hundredths or 0·13 of a pound.

Exercise 11

Copy and complete these sentences. The first two have been done for you.

1. 7p is the same as £0·07

2. 23p is the same as £0·23

3. 9p is the same as £0·0*

4. 5p is the same as £0·**

5. 8p is the same as £0·**

6. 6p is the same as £0·**

7. 16p is the same as £0·**

8. 27p is the same as £0·**

9. 43p is the same as £0·**

10. 61p is the same as £0·**

11. * p is the same as £0·02

12. * p is the same as £0·04

13. * p is the same as £0·08

14. ** p is the same as £0·16

15. ** p is the same as £0·35

16. ** p is the same as £0·61

Exercise 1

In this simple code each number stands for a letter.

The code

A	C	E	H	I	S	T
1	2	3	4	5	6	7

Use the code to find out what these messages mean.

1. 6,3,3   7,4,3   2,1,7

2. 4,3   5,6   1   2,4,3,1,7

3. 7,4,1,7   5,6   4,5,6   2,1,7

4. 5   4,1,7,3   7,4,1,7   4,1,7

5. 7,1,6,7,3   7,4,3   7,3,1

Put these sentences into code, using the code above.

6. This is his.   **7.** She sat a test.

8. She has a chat.   **9.** He hit his chest.

10. Test the set.

Exercise 2

Here is a map of enemy territory. Copy it and de-code the information on it.

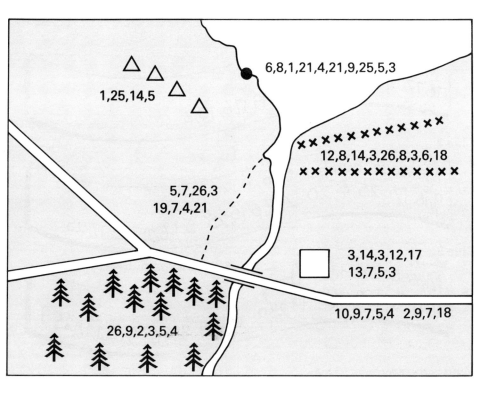

Code

1	G	14	N
2	R	15	V
3	E	16	J
4	T	17	Y
5	S	18	D
6	L	19	P
7	A	20	X
8	I	21	H
9	O	22	W
10	C	23	Q
11	Z	24	K
12	M	25	U
13	B	26	F

Exercise 3

One of these people is a spy.
De-code the clues and find which one is the spy.

	The code												
A	B	C	D	E	F	G	H	I	J	K	L	M
6	19	14	3	17	13	5	16	8	22	15	1	7
N	O	P	Q	R	S	T	U	V	W	X	Y	Z
11	12	4	18	10	25	9	23	21	2	24	20	26

Jim   Bob   Tom   Boris   Harry   James   Jon   Emma

Clue 1.

Message number one
16,17 16,6,25 11,12 19,17,6,10,3

Clue 2.

Message number two
9,16,17 25,4,20 2,17,6,10,25 5,1,6,25,25,17,25

Clue 3.

Message number three
16,17 8,25 9,6,1,1 19,23,9 11,12,9 9,16,17 9,6,1,1,17,25,9

Who is the spy?

A	B	C	D	E	F	G	H	I
20	6	11	16	22	30	8	17	5

	J	K	L	M	N	O	P	Q
	46	34	12	27	15	9	14	24

R	S	T	U	V	W	X	Y	Z
40	7	13	4	2	23	29	10	19

Exercise 4

How did Bill get his black eye?
De-code the message below and find out.

$(14 + 3), (11 + 11)$

$(19 - 8), (34 - 14), (24 - 12), (32 - 20), (26 - 4), (21 - 5)$

$(12 \div 2), (20 \div 4), (24 \div 3)$

$(6 \times 5), (5 \times 8), (2 \times 11), (4 \times 4)$

$(1 + 19)$

$(14 - 7), (25 - 11), (26 - 17), (14 - 1), (20 - 7), (40 - 30)$

$(4 \times 3), (3 + 17), (31 - 21), (4 \times 5), (18 \div 3), (11 - 2), (12 \div 3), (2 + 11)$

Exercise 5

Using the code above, find out what the bear is thinking to himself.

13,17,22 ~ 6,22,20,40 ~
8,9,22,7 ~
17,4,15,13,5,15,8.

40,22,20,16,10 ~ 13,9 ~
12,22,20,14 ~ 9,15 ~
17,5,7 ~ 14,40,22,10.

23,17,20,13 ~
13,40,22,20,13 ~
13,9,15,5,8,17,13?

Exercise 6

Answer these questions about yourself. Put your answers into code using the code at the top of the page.

1. What is your first name?

2. What is your favourite colour?

3. Do you support a football team?

4. Which pop group or singer do you like?

5. Have you any pets at home?

Review 1

A. Fractions

What fraction is shaded in each of these shapes?

1. 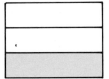 **2.**   **3.**   **4.** 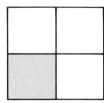 **5.**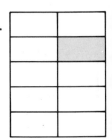

Match these fraction numbers with the correct drawings below.

a. $\frac{2}{3}$ **b.** $\frac{3}{4}$ **c.** $\frac{2}{5}$ **d.** $\frac{4}{5}$ **e.** $\frac{3}{10}$

6. 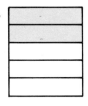 **7.**  **8.** 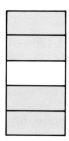 **9.**  **10.**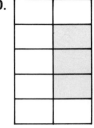

Answer these four questions about each drawing below.

a. How many parts are there?
b. What fraction is each part?
c. What fraction is shaded?
d. What fraction is unshaded?

11. 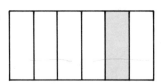 **12.**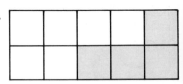

B. Triangles

There are 180° in a triangle. Find the missing angle in each triangle.

1.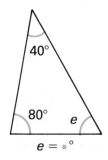

$e = *°$

2.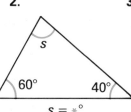

$s = *°$

3.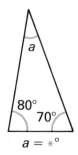

$a = *°$

4.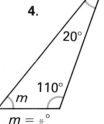

$m = *°$

5.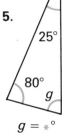

$g = *°$

C. Decimal measurement

1. The toy soldier is
4 cm and 8 tenths long.
This can be written as 4·8 cm.

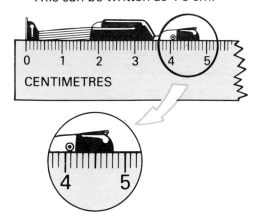

What are the lengths of these objects?

2. This stamp is _____ cm long.

3. This match is _____ cm long.

4. This spark plug is _____ cm long.

5. This clip is _____ cm long.

Measure these lines accurately.

6. ├───────────────────────┤

7. ├────────────────────────────┤

8. ├──────────┤

9. ├──────────────────────────┤

10. ├──────┤

D. Time

How many minutes have passed between the times shown on each pair of clocks?

1.

2.

How many hours and minutes have passed between the times shown on each pair of clocks?

3.

4.

Copy and complete these sentences, a.m. or p.m.

5. 06.00 is the same as 6 _____

6. 13.00 is the same as 1 _____

7. 18.15 is the same as 6.15 _____

8. 09.00 is the same as 9 _____

9. 11.00 is the same as 11 _____

10. 22.30 is the same as 10.30 _____

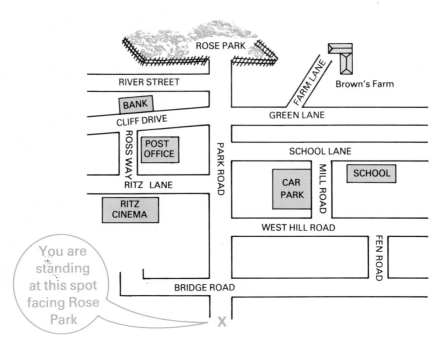

Exercise 1

Look at the map above. Imagine you are standing at 'X'.

1. Which road leads to Rose Park?
2. Which road is second on the left?
3. Which road is first on the left?
4. Which road is third on the right?
5. Which road is fourth on the right?
6. Where will you be if you take the second turning on the right and then the first on the left?
7. Where will you be if you take the first turning on the right and then the first on the left?
8. Where will you be if you take the second turning on the left and then the first on the right?

How to give directions:
The way to the Ritz Cinema: Walk up Park Road. Take the second turning on the left. The cinema is on your left.

Exercise 2

Look at the map above. Imagine you are standing at 'X'.

1. Give directions to the bank.
2. Give directions to Brown's Farm.
3. Give directions to the school.
4. Give directions to the Post Office.
5. Starting at the Ritz Cinema, give directions to the school.
6. Starting at the school, give directions to Brown's Farm.
7. Starting at the Post Office, give directions to the car park.

Here is the block of flats at Gladstone House.
A window has been broken in one of the flats.
The caretaker says it is the window that
is 2 from the left and 3 levels up.

We can describe the position of any window.

Mr Cross is selling his flat. His window
is 1 from the left and 2 levels up.

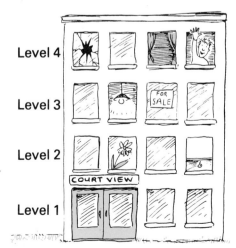

Exercise 3

1. What will you find in the window 2 from the left, 2 levels up?

2. What will you find in the window 5 from the left, 4 levels up?

3. What will you find in the window 1 from the left, 3 levels up?

4. What will you find in the window 3 from the left, 4 levels up?

5. What will you find in the window 5 from the left, 2 levels up?

6. What will you find in the window 1 from the left, 4 levels up?

7. What will you find in the window 3 from the left, 3 levels up?

8. What will you find in the window 4 from the left, 2 levels up?

Now look at the flats at Court View.
Write down these locations.

9. The window with the light.

10. The window with the curtains.

11. The window with the flower.

12. The window with blinds.

13. The window with the boy waving.

14. The broken window.

15. The window of the flat that
is for sale.

Exercise 4

The seating plan in the green box is for the economy cabin, on a flight to New York.

Mr. Radia has a seat booked. His seat is in column G, row 12. His ticket will have G12 written on it.

Copy out the passenger list. Put each passenger's seat number beside the name.

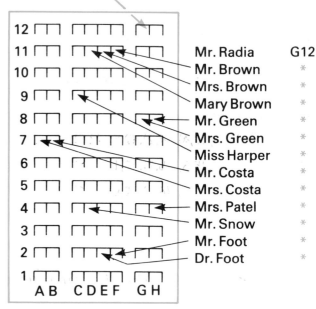

Mr. Radia	G12
Mr. Brown	*
Mrs. Brown	*
Mary Brown	*
Mr. Green	*
Mrs. Green	*
Miss Harper	*
Mr. Costa	*
Mrs. Costa	*
Mrs. Patel	*
Mr. Snow	*
Mr. Foot	*
Dr. Foot	*

Exercise 5

These passengers arrive late.
Give the name of the passenger next to them on Flight AT142 to New York.

1. Mr. Smart is given seat E4.   **2.** Miss Jay is given seat G4.

3. Mr. Cross is given seat H12.   **4.** Mrs. Bath is given seat D2.

5. Ms. Cole is given seat D9.   **6.** Dr. Lee is given seat C11.

Exercise 6

Here is the seating plan for the First Class cabin on the New York flight. Copy it out and show where each passenger is sitting using arrows.

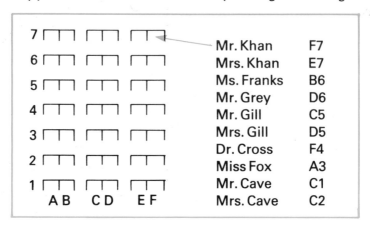

Mr. Khan	F7
Mrs. Khan	E7
Ms. Franks	B6
Mr. Grey	D6
Mr. Gill	C5
Mrs. Gill	D5
Dr. Cross	F4
Miss Fox	A3
Mr. Cave	C1
Mrs. Cave	C2

Exercise 7

Can you spell out the tongue-twister shown by the coordinates below?

Replace each pair of numbers by the correct letter.

Remember: The first number is 'across'.
The second number is 'up'.

The first coordinate is (6,1) which is 'r'.

(6,1), (7,6), (1,3)

(5,3), (2,6), (3,4), (7,4), (4,2), (7,6), (2,7)

(6,5), (2,6), (1,2), (5,3), (8,1), (3,1)

(1,2), (7,6), (7,0), (1,5), (4,2), (2,6), (6,1)

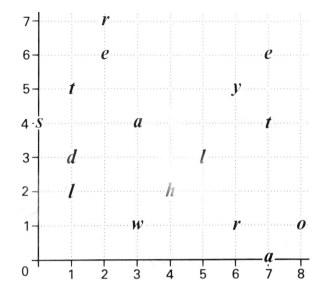

Exercise 8

Look carefully at this map. Then answer these questions.

Write down what you will find at

1. the coordinates (8,6)
2. the coordinates (1,9)
3. the coordinates (9,8)
4. the coordinates (4,5)
5. the coordinates (2,4)

Give the coordinates for

6. the roundabout.
7. the lighthouse.
8. the dock.
9. the station.
10. the boat.
11. the level crossing.
12. Sty Farm.
13. the castle.
14. Pond Farm.
15. the bridge.

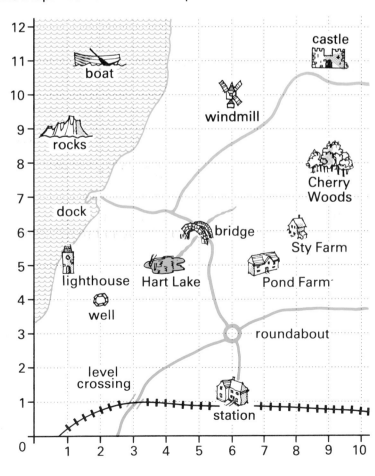

Grids

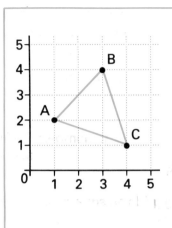

This is a grid. On the grid there is a triangle.

The corners of the triangle are called A,B,C.

Starting from 0,   A is 1 across and 2 up.
B is 3 across and 4 up.
C is 4 across and 1 up.

To save time, we write the positions like this:
A(1,2) B(3,4) C(4,1)

These numbers are called coordinates.
The first number is 'across'.
The second number is 'up'.

Exercise 9

Copy each grid and answer the questions.

1. a. What is the position of R? (___ , ___)

b. What is the position of A? (___ , ___)

c. What is the position of Y? (___ , ___)

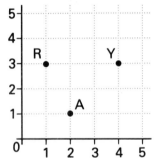

2. a. What are the coordinates of P?

b. What are the coordinates of A?

c. What are the coordinates of T?

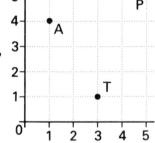

3. Write in your book the coordinates of each letter on the grid.

D (___ , ___)

Y (___ , ___)

N (___ , ___)

A (___ , ___)

M (___ , ___)

I (___ , ___)

T (___ , ___)

E (___ , ___)

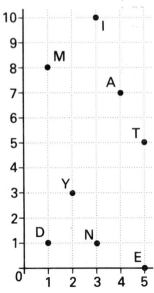

4. Write the coordinates of each letter.

M (___ , ___)   A (___ , ___)   T (___ , ___)

H (___ , ___)   S (___ , ___)   W (___ , ___)

O (___ , ___)   R (___ , ___)   K (___ , ___)

I (___ , ___)   N (___ , ___)   G (___ , ___)

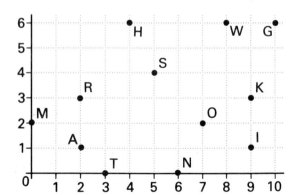

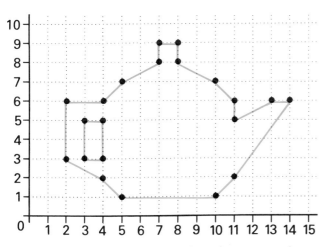

This picture has been drawn using the following coordinates.

(14,6), (11,2), (10,1), (5,1), (4,2), (2,3), (2,6), (4,6), (5,7), (7,8), (7,9), (8,9), (8,8), (10,7), (11,6), (11,5), (13,6), (14,6)

(4,3), (4,5), (3,5), (3,3), (4,3)

Remember: the first number is 'across', the second number is 'up'.

Exercise 10 Draw out the following grids on squared paper. Plot the coordinates. Then draw a picture by joining up the points in the order you plotted them.

1. (10,3), (9,1), (3,1), (1,3), (10,3), (6,11), (6,3), (5,4), (1,4), (6,10)

2. (12,13), (9,12), (8,13), (7,17), (7,19), (6,20), (5,20), (4,19), (1,17), (5,18), (6,17), (7,11), (7,9), (10,7), (10,2), (7,1), (11,1), (10,2), (10,7), (12,8), (14,9), (15,11), (15,16), (14,12), (12,13).

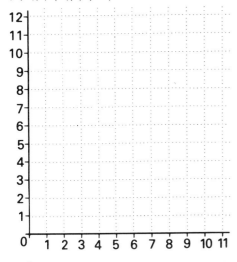

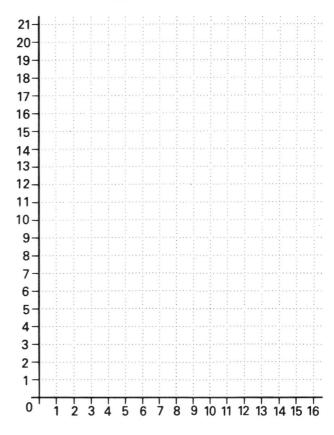

3. (2,3), (2,1), (1,1), (1,6), (2,6), (2,4), (3,6), (4,6), (3,3), (4,1), (3,1), (2,3)
   (5,1), (6,1), (6,4), (5,4), (5,1)   (5,6), (6,6), (6,5), (5,5), (5,6)
   (9,2), (9,4), (10,4), (10,5), (9,5), (9,6), (8,6), (8,5), (7,5), (7,4), (8,4), (8,2), (9,1), (10,2), (10,3), (9,2).

Exercise 11

1. **a.** Give four pairs of coordinates which are on the green line.

   b. Give four pairs of coordinates which are to the left of the line.

   c. Give four pairs of coordinates which are to the right of the line.

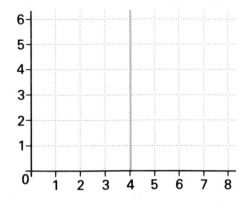

2. **a.** What are the coordinates of the corners A, B, C and D?

   b. Give five pairs of coordinates which are outside the rectangle.

   c. Give four pairs of coordinates which are inside the rectangle.

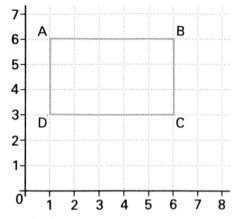

3. **a.** Give four pairs of coordinates which are on the circle.

   b. Give four pairs of coordinates which are outside the circle.

   c. Give three pairs of coordinates which are inside the circle.

   d. What are the coordinates of the centre of the circle?

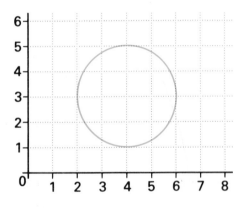

4. **a.** Give four pairs of coordinates which are above the green line.

   b. Give four pairs of coordinates which are below the green line.

   c. Give four pairs of coordinates which are on the green line

   d. Write down four more pairs of coordinates which would be on the green line if it was drawn longer.

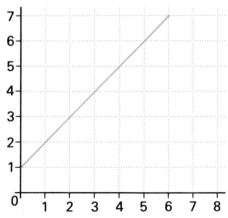

Section 9   **Distance**

When you measure a distance, it is necessary to choose suitable units.
For example:

In a town...	on a lawn...	is a slice of bread...	with an ant on it.
	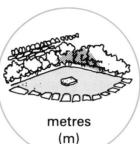	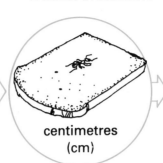	
kilometres (km)	metres (m)	centimetres (cm)	millimetres (mm)

The choice of unit depends on the size or distance to be measured.

For example:

The smallest adult fish, the Dwarf Goby is about 9 mm long (or $\frac{3}{10}$ inch long).

The world's shortest male dwarf, Calvin Phillips, was only 67 cm tall (or just over 2 ft. tall).

The world's highest waterfall, The Angel Falls in Venezuela is 972 m in height (or over half a mile high).

In 1978 Hans Mulkin crawled 2560 km (or 1600 miles) to see the President in Washington. Sadly, the President was too busy.

Exercise 1

Decide which units you would use to measure these distances.

1. The length of your foot.
   millimetre – centimetre – metre

2. The height of your house.
   millimetre – centimetre – metre

3. The length of an eye lash.
   millimetre – centimetre – metre

4. The distance around the world.
   centimetre – metre – kilometre

5. The distance around your head.
   millimetre – centimetre – metre

6. The width of a pencil.
   millimetre – centimetre – metre

7. The distance from your school to the South Pole.
   centimetre – metre – kilometre

8. The distance from your home to school.
   millimetre – metre – kilometre

9. The distance around your wrist.
   centimetre – metre – kilometre

10. Your height.
    millimetre – centimetre – kilometre

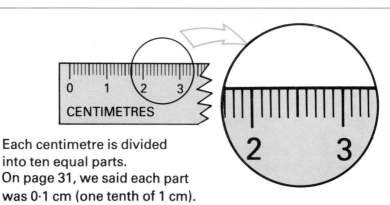

Each centimetre is divided
into ten equal parts.
On page 31, we said each part
was 0·1 cm (one tenth of 1 cm).

Each of these parts is also called 1 millimetre (1 mm).

0·1 cm = 1 mm   1 cm = 10 mm

Exercise 2

2 cm = 20 mm

2·5 cm = 25 mm

Change these centimetre measurements into millimetre measurements.

1. 1 cm = *   **2.** 2 cm = *   **3.** 4 cm = *   **4.** 5 cm = *

5. 7 cm = *   **6.** 2·5 cm = *   **7.** 3·5 cm = *   **8.** 6·5 cm = *

9. 4·2 cm = *   **10.** 3·4 cm = * **11.** 9·7 cm = * **12.** 10 cm = *

Exercise 3

80 mm = 8 cm

15 mm = 1·5 cm

Change these millimetre measurements into centimetre measurements.

1. 80 mm = *   **2.** 90 mm = *   **3.** 20 mm = *   **4.** 40 mm = *

5. 30 mm = *   **6.** 60 mm = *   **7.** 15 mm = *   **8.** 25 mm = *

9. 47 mm = *   **10.** 92 mm = *   **11.** 87 mm = *   **12.** 100 mm = *

Exercise 4

In each of the drawings, guess which of the lettered lines is the
longest. Now check your guesses with a ruler and complete the table.

Line	cm
a	
b	
c	
d	
e	
f	
g	

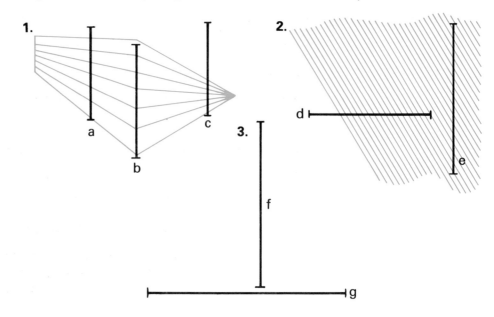

Measurements in metres

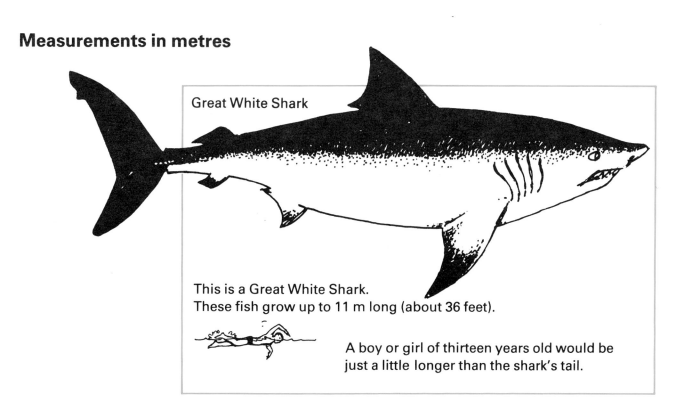

Great White Shark

This is a Great White Shark.
These fish grow up to 11 m long (about 36 feet).

A boy or girl of thirteen years old would be
just a little longer than the shark's tail.

Exercise 5

Guess the lengths or heights of these animals. When you have written your
answers, check them with the world records† shown below.

1. The largest python. 2. The largest crocodile ever known to have lived.

3. The tallest giraffe. 4. The largest Blue Whale.

5. The longest dinosaur. 6. The longest lobster caught.

Remember: there are 100 centimetres in 1 metre.   1 m = 100 cm or 100 cm = 1 m.

Exercise 6

2 m = 200 cm

4·2 m = 420 cm

Change these metre measurements to centimetre measurements.

1. 1 m = *   2. 2 m = *   3. 4 m = *   4. 3 m = *

5. 6 m = *   6. 8 m = *   7. 9 m = *   8. 4·2 m = *

9. 5·5 m = *   10. 1·6 m = *   11. 2·2 m = *   12. 7·6 m = *

Exercise 7

100 cm = 1 m

750 cm = 7·5 m

Change these centimetre measurements into metre measurements.

1. 100 cm = *   2. 200 cm = *   3. 500 cm = *   4. 700 cm = *

5. 900 cm = *   6. 800 cm = *   7. 400 cm = *   8. 750 cm = *

9. 420 cm = *   10. 160 cm = *   11. 370 cm = *   12. 50 cm = *

1: 10 m long (33 ft); 2: 16 m long (52 ft); 3: 6 m tall (20 ft);
4: 33·5 m long (110 ft) 5: 26·5 m long (87 ft); 6: 1·0 m long (3½ ft); ,

†World records for sizes of animals.

Section 10   **Sorting into sets**

A set is a group or collection of things.

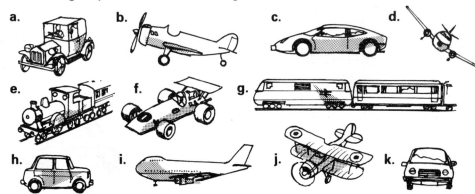

Exercise 1

Draw three set rings like these and label them.

     trains   aeroplanes   cars

Sort the objects above into the rings.
Put the letter for each object above into the correct ring.

Exercise 2

These sets have been sorted incorrectly.

    months   days   seasons

Redraw the three set rings and put the words in their correct places.

Exercise 3

Draw three separate set rings and label them 'cricket players', 'basketball players' and 'swimmers'.
From the data below, fill in the names on the rings, then answer the questions.

John only plays cricket. Peter plays cricket and swims. Jane swims and so does Ray. Ali plays basketball and cricket. Errol only likes swimming. Rose plays basketball, but Kenneth plays basketball and cricket.

1. Who plays basketball and cricket?   **2.** Who swims and plays cricket?

3. How many people play two sports?   **4.** How many play only one sport?

Belonging to more than one set

These people can be sorted into two different set rings as shown below.

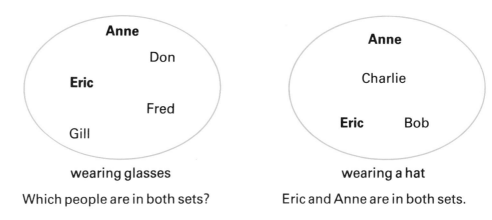

wearing glasses

Which people are in both sets?

wearing a hat

Eric and Anne are in both sets.

The two set rings can be re-drawn like this:

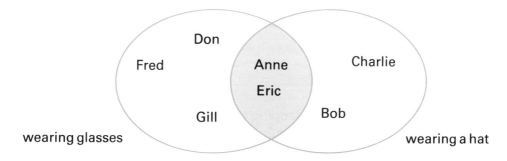

From this diagram we can see that Eric and Anne belong in both sets. In other words, Eric and Anne wear both glasses and a hat.

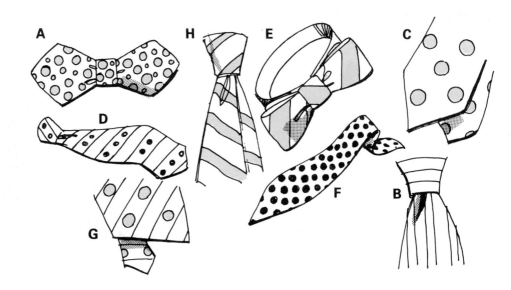

Exercise 4

1. Draw two set rings like these.
   Label them 'spotty ties' and 'striped ties'.
   Sort the ties into the two sets.

2. Put the letters for each tie into
   the correct space.

3. If a tie is spotty and striped,
   its letter should go into the shaded
   area belonging to both sets.

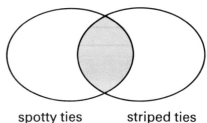

spotty ties   striped ties

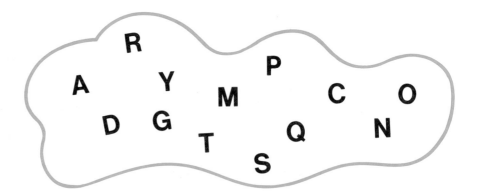

Exercise 5

1. Draw two over-lapping or intersecting set rings as you did in Exercise 4.
2. Label the two rings 'curved letters' and 'straight-line letters'.
3. Sort the letters into two sets:
   a. those made only from straight lines.
   b. those made only from curves.
4. Letters formed from both curves and straight lines should go into the
   over-lapping area.

Understanding set rings

Exercise 6   Answer these questions about each diagram.
The first one has been done for you.

1.

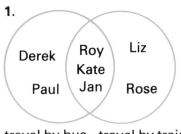

travel by bus   travel by train

a. Who travels by train only?
   Answer: Liz and Rose.

b. Who travels by bus only?
   Answer: Derek and Paul.

c. Who travels by bus and train?
   Answer: Roy, Kate and Jan.

d. How many people travel altogether?
   Answer: 7 people.

2.

wear bow ties   wear straight ties

a. Who wears a bow tie only?

b. How many wear both types of tie?

c. What type of tie does Adrian wear?

d. How many people wear a straight tie?

3.

black dogs   white dogs

a. How many dogs are there altogether?

b. How many dogs are black and white?

c. Which dogs are only black?

d. Which dogs are part or fully white?

4.

John   Pam   Maria
Tracy   Dave
        Mick   Kevin

chess club   darts club

a. How many people play darts?

b. What game does Kevin play?

c. Who plays both games?

d. Does Tracy play both games?

5.

Errol   Ali   Frank
Linda   Fred
Roy   Paula

school lunch   go to youth club

a. Who stays for school lunch?

b. Who has a school lunch and goes to youth club?

c. Does Paula have school lunch?

d. How many people are there altogether?

The set of numbers on the left are of two different types:
- **a.** those numbers in the '2-times table'.
- **b.** those numbers in the '3-times table'. This is shown by the two set rings on the right.

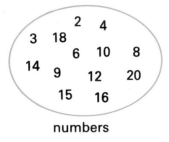

numbers

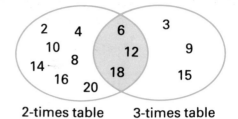

2-times table   3-times table

Note that some of the numbers are in both tables, so they go into the over-lap: they are then in both set rings.

Exercise 7

Copy and complete each diagram.
Make sure you put all the numbers somewhere in the two set rings.
Take care with the overlap area where the two rings intersect.
You may need to look in some multiplication tables.

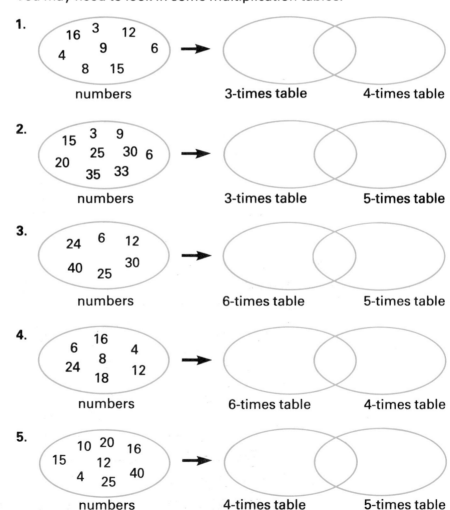

Review 2

A. Coordinates

Give the coordinates for the letters marked on the grid.

1. a is at (___ , ___)

2. b is at (___ , ___)

3. c is at (___ , ___)

4. d is at (___ , ___)

5. e is at (___ , ___)

6. f is at (___ , ___)

What do you find at these coordinates?

7. (2,4) = *

8. (9,1) = *

9. (1,9) = *

10. (10,6) = *

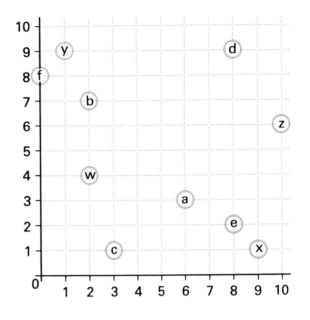

B. Codes

1. Use this code to find out what message is written below.

    4,5,9   2,6,4,4,3

    3,5,2,2,6,8   2,6,4,4,3

$e = 5$	$o = 6$	$y = 3$
$d = 9$	$r = 4$	
$l = 2$	$w = 8$	

2. Here is a code that uses coordinates.

Look at the grid on the right.

Each pair of coordinates below will give you a letter on the grid.

  (2,4) (9,5) (7,2) (1,1)

  (5,3) (5,6) (0,2) (8,0)

  (2,3) (9,3) (10,2)

  (6,1) (9,3) (7,2) (0,2)

  (6,1) (3,5) (7,4) (10,6) (4,1)

Can you read the message?

C. Angles

Remember there are 180 ° in a straight angle.
Find the missing angle.

1.

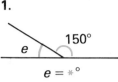

150°

e

$e = *°$

2.

g 70°

$g = *°$

3.

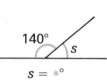

140° s

$s = *°$

4.

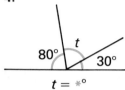

80° t 30°

$t = *°$

5.

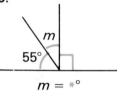

m

55°

$m = *°$

D. Triangles

Remember there are 180 ° in a triangle.
Find the missing angle.

1.

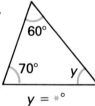

60°

70° y

$y = *°$

2.

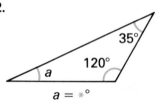

35°

120° a

$a = *°$

3.

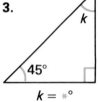

k

45°

$k = *°$

4. Use a ruler and protractor to draw this triangle.

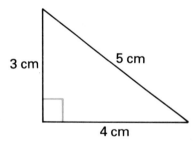

3 cm 5 cm

4 cm

5. Use a ruler and a pair of compasses to draw this triangle.

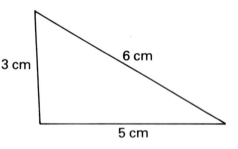

3 cm 6 cm

5 cm

E. Problems

1. How much greater is 50 than 35?

2. How many 10p pieces are there in £1·20?

3. Put these units of measurement in order of size, beginning with the smallest: metre – millimetre – kilometre – centimetre.

4. Put these numbers in order of size, beginning with the smallest: 251 – 189 – 991 – 1001 – 300.

5. If one minibus holds 15 people, how many would 4 minibuses hold?

F. Time

1. An aircraft takes off from Gatwick at 1 p.m. It lands in Paris at 2.17 p.m. How long does the journey take?

2. A train leaves Glasgow at 7.30 a.m. It arrives in Birmingham at 11.45 a.m. How long does the journey take?

3. A ferry leaves Dover at 11 a.m. and arrives in Calais at 1.15 p.m. How long does the journey take?

4. Jenny takes 15 minutes to write one page of work. How long would it take her to write six pages?

5. A bus arrives at the bus stop once every ten minutes. How many buses would arrive in one hour?

Look at these bus times. They are given in 24-hour time.

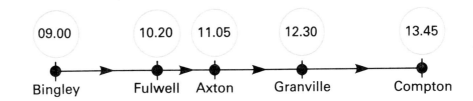

Write down how long the journey takes

6. from Bingley to Fulwell   7. from Fulwell to Axton

8. from Axton to Granville   9. from Fulwell to Compton

10. How long does the total journey take?

G. Distance

1. Use the scale on the right to find the height of:

   a. the gas holder

   b. the TV tower

   c. Nell's Store

   d. the Airways Building

   e. the Weston Bank

2. What is the difference in height between Nell's Store and the Weston Bank?

3. What is the difference in height between the Weston Bank and the gas holder?

4. What is the difference in height between the TV tower and the Airways Building?

5. What is the difference in height between Nell's Store and the TV tower?

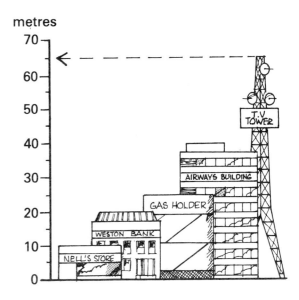

H. Sets

1. Draw three large set rings like these, and label them.

tools   clothes   food

Here is a collection of items.
Write the letter of each item correctly in one of the rings you have drawn.

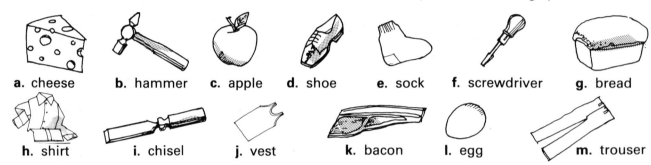

a. cheese   **b.** hammer   **c.** apple   **d.** shoe   **e.** sock   **f.** screwdriver   **g.** bread

h. shirt   **i.** chisel   **j.** vest   **k.** bacon   **l.** egg   **m.** trouser

2. Look carefully at what these people are wearing.

Paul   Diane   Hilda   Basil

Copy these rings, then put the names of the people in the correct places.
Some names may be in the coloured area because they belong to both sets.

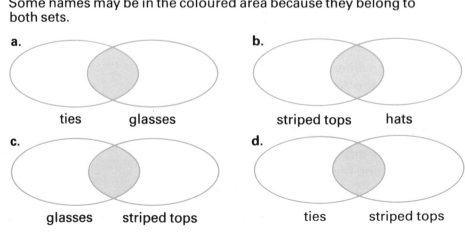

a.
ties   glasses

b.
striped tops   hats

c.
glasses   striped tops

d.
ties   striped tops

Graphs

Graphs are used to display information so that it can be clearly understood.

Toby's parents have measured his height every year on his birthday.
They stand him against the garden wall and mark his height.

Here is Toby on his tenth birthday.

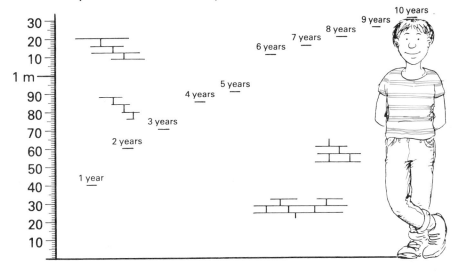

This information can be easily displayed on a graph.

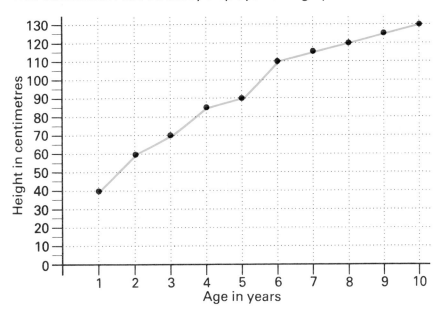

Exercise 1

1. How tall was Toby when he was
   a. one year old   b. six years old   c. five years old
   d. four years old   e. nine years old   f. ten years old?

2. How old was Toby when he was   a. 70 cm tall   b. 115 cm tall?

3. How much did Toby grow between   a. years 1 and 2   b. years 5 and 6?

Class 3M are writing a project on the human heart.
They are going to see how the heart beat changes after hard exercise.

Pauline does 'step-ups' on a stool for one minute.
She then sits down and takes her pulse rate
every minute. Here are the results.

	Number of heart beats
In the 1st minute	120
In the 2nd minute	90
In the 3rd minute	85
In the 4th minute	75
In the 5th minute	70

Look at the graph below. It shows how her pulse rate changed
during 5 minutes.

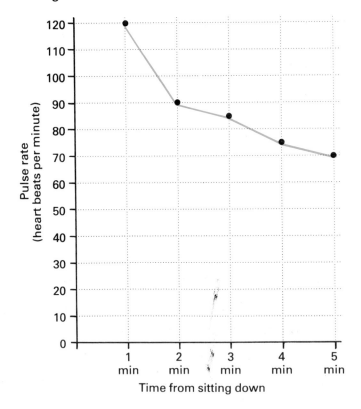

Exercise 2

1. What is the highest number of heart beats on the graph?

2. What is her pulse rate after 2 min?

3. What is her pulse rate after 4 min?

4. What is her pulse rate after 3 min?

5. How long is it until her pulse rate drops to 70 beats per min?

Exercise 3

Roy is saving some of his pocket money.
He uses a graph to record his savings.

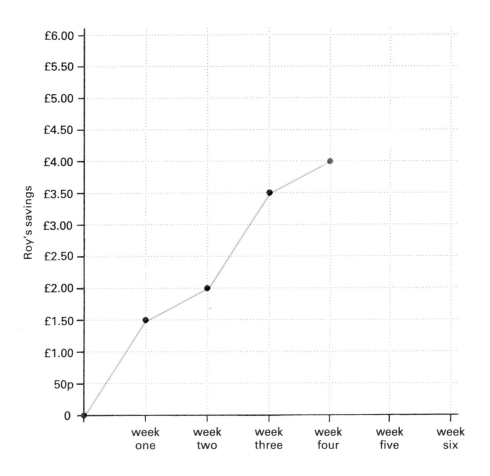

1. How much did he save during week one?

2. How much had he saved by week two?

3. How much had he saved by week three?

4. How much had he saved by week four?

5. How much did he add to his savings between week two
   and week three?

6. How much did he add to his savings between week three
   and week four?

7. Roy saved 50p in week five, so his total savings were
   £4.50. Copy the graph above and plot this point.

8. His aunt gave him £1.00 in week six. He then had
   £5.50. Plot this point on your graph.

Exercise 1

The Speedee Delivery van carries goods from Axford to the local shops. Here is the map the driver uses.

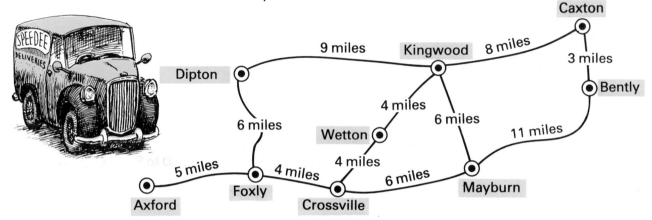

Answer these questions about this map.

1. Foxly is ___ miles from Mayburn.

2. Dipton is ___ miles from Axford.

3. Mayburn is ___ miles from Caxton.

4. The van goes from Axford to Foxly, Crossville and Wetton. How far has it travelled?

5. From Wetton the van goes to Kingwood, Mayburn and Bently. How far is this journey?

6. From Bently the van goes to Caxton, Kingwood and Dipton. How far is this journey?

7. How far is Crossville from Caxton by the shortest route?

8. How far is Dipton from Bently by the shortest route?

9. Give directions for a journey from Foxly to Caxton.

10. Copy these sign posts and fill in the missing information.

a. The signpost in Wetton

b. The signpost in Bently

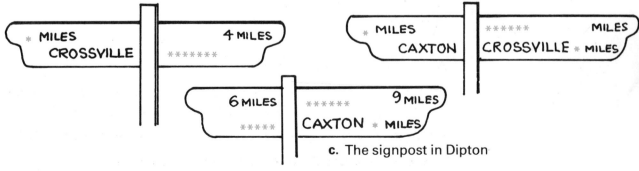

c. The signpost in Dipton

Exercise 2

Jo entered for the Cresswell car rally.
The distance shows her start-time at A, the time at each check-point,
and the time at the finish F.

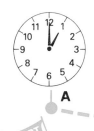 **A**  **B**  **C**  **D**  **E**  **F**

START

FINISH

1. How long did she take for each stage?
   a. A to B   **b.** B to C   **c.** C to D   **d.** D to E   **e.** E to F

2. How long did the first two stages take?

3. How long did the last three stages take?

4. What was the total time taken from start to finish?

5. Which stage took the shortest time?

Exercise 3

1. Jo takes part in another rally. The rally starts at P and finishes at V.

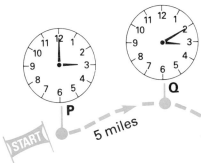 **P** **Q** 5 miles 7 miles

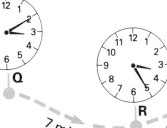 **R** 6 miles

 **S** 13 miles **T**

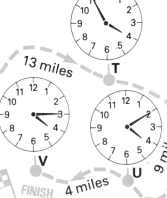 **V** **U** 9 miles 4 miles

FINISH

1. Write down the distance for
   each stage
   a. PQ   **b.** QR   **c.** RS   **d.** ST   **e.** TU   **f.** UV

2. What was the total distance from start to finish?

3. How long did Jo take   **a.** from P to Q   **b.** on the second stage
                              c. from P to R   **d.** from Q to T?

4. Which stage took   **a.** the shortest time   **b.** the longest time?

5. How long did it take Jo to complete the first 18 miles?

Travel graphs

A more useful way of showing the time and distance travelled on a journey is by means of a travel graph.

Time is shown horizontally.

Distance is shown vertically.

This graph shows a rally car travelling from A to G.

Check points A to G show the distance and time from the start.

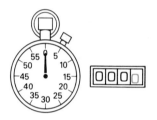

The stop-watch and the trip-meter start when the car starts.

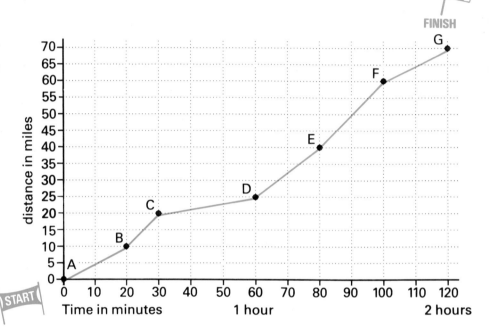

Exercise 4

1. How long did the car take to reach check-point B?

2. What was the distance from check-point A to check-point B?

3. How far has the car travelled between check-points A and C?

4. How long did the car take to travel from A to D?

5. How far did the car travel between C and E?

6. How far did the car travel in the first hour?

7. Which check-point did the car reach in the first 80 minutes?

8. How long did it take to reach check-point F?

9. How many miles did the car travel between check-points C and G?

10. How many miles was the total journey?

11. How many hours did the total journey take?

12. Which stage of the journey took the most time?
    a. A to B   **b.** B to C   **c.** C to D   **d.** D to E   **e.** E to F   **f.** F to G

Exercise 5

This travel graph is incomplete.

The graph should show a journey from A to F.

The data required to complete the graph is shown in the table below.

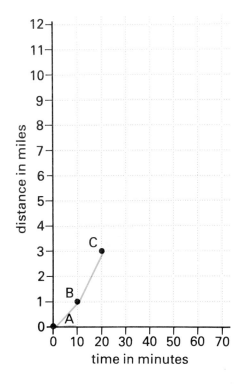

stage of journey	distance of stage	time taken
from A to B	1 mile	10 minutes
from B to C	2 miles	10 minutes
from C to D	4 miles	20 minutes
from D to E	3 miles	10 minutes
from E to F	2 miles	20 minutes
Totals	12 miles	70 minutes

1. Copy the graph in your book.

2. Study the table and then complete the graph.
Label each stage of the journey. The next stage goes from C to D.

3. Write down the type of transport that you think made the journey.

  a. The Concorde airliner   **b.** A bicycle

  c. A sports car   **d.** A high-speed train

Exercise 6

Rosie went for a cycle ride. She measured the time and the distance that she travelled for each stage of her ride.
Here are her results.

  a. Rosie cycled the first 4 miles in 10 minutes.

  b. She took 30 minutes to cycle the next 2 miles.

  c. Rosie cycled the next 2 miles in 20 minutes.

  d. She finished her cycle ride 30 minutes later after cycling another 2 miles.

1. Make a table similar to the one in Exercise 5.

2. Draw a graph to show Rosie's journey.

Exercise 7

Here is a map of a train journey from Penzance to London.
The train leaves Penzance at 9.30 a.m. and arrives in London at 1.30 p.m.

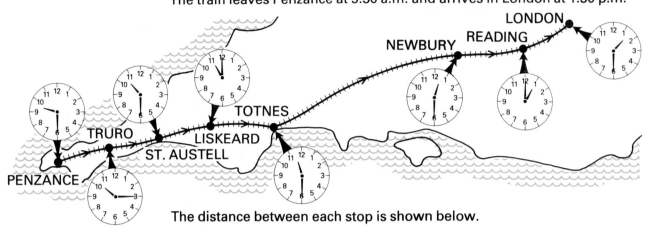

The distance between each stop is shown below.

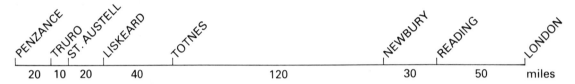

The travel graph for this journey is shown below: it is incomplete.

1. Make a table showing the distance between each station and the time taken between each station.

2. Copy the graph shown below in your book.

3. Complete the graph showing each station in the correct place. The first three stations have been marked for you.

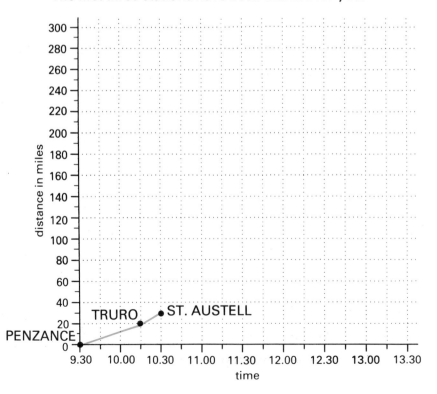

Barry goes for a walk. Here is a graph of his journey.

He walks a total of 3 miles in one hour.

After 30 minutes, he stops for a rest.
The rest lasted 10 minutes.

When Barry is resting, the distance remains the same, but time still keeps ticking by. . .

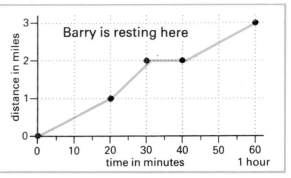

Barry is resting here

Exercise 8

These travel graphs show three different journeys.

a.

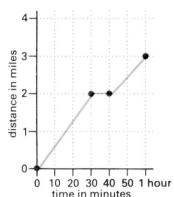

b.

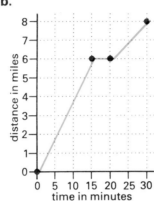

c.

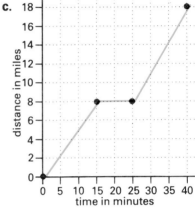

Answer these five questions about each of the graphs.

1. What distance was the journey?

2. How much time did it take?

3. How long did the stop last for?

4. What distance had been travelled before the stop?

5. How much time had passed before the stop?

Exercise 9

Look at the travel graph of Pam's cycle ride.

1. How long did the first 4 miles take?

2. How far had Pam cycled in the first 25 minutes?

3. How much time passed before the first stop?

4. How many minutes did Pam rest for at Point A?

5. Which was the longest stop: A, B or C?

6. How long was the longest stop?

7. When did Pam stop to rest at point C?

8. For how long did Pam cycle between stops A and B?

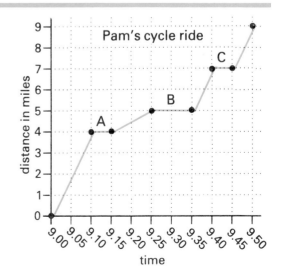

Pam's cycle ride

Exercise 1

For these problems, four calculations are shown.
Only one of the calculations leads to the correct answer.
Find the correct calculation and solve the problem.

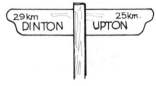

1. From the signpost it is 29 km to Dinton and 25 km to Upton. How far is it from Dinton to Upton?

     a.   25   **b.**   29   **c.**   29   **d.** 25$\overline{)29}$

          $-\,29$ $+\,25$ $-\,25$

2. Mr Webb plants 4 rows of daffodils with 8 bulbs in each row. How many bulbs has he planted?

     a. $8 + 4$ **b.** $8 - 4$ **c.** $8 \div 4$ **d.** 4×8

3. If Mr Webb had to plant 48 bulbs, how many rows would he need to plant if he still wanted 8 bulbs in a row?

     a. 48×8 **b.** $48 \div 8$ **c.** $48 + 8$ **d.** $48 - 8$

4. There were 67 people on the bus. After the bus stopped, there were 29 people left on board. How many people got off the bus?

     a. $67 - 29$ **b.** $67 + 29$ **c.** $29 - 67$ **d.** $67 \div 29$

5. The train is 262 m long. If 77 m is out of the tunnel, how much is still inside?

     a. $262 + 77$ **b.** $77 + 262$ **c.** $77 - 262$ **d.** $262 - 77$

6. In the Rex Cinema there are seats for 96 people. How many rows are there if there are 8 seats in each row?

     a. $96 \div 8$ **b.** 96×8 **c.** $96 - 8$ **d.** $8 + 96$

7. If 237 queued to watch the film at the Rex Cinema, how many would not be allowed in the cinema?

     a. 96×237 **b.** $237 - 96$ **c.** $237 + 96$ **d.** $96 + 237$

8. The cinema was rebuilt. It now has 9 rows with 25 seats in each row. How many people will the cinema hold?

     a. $25 + 9$ **b.** $25 \div 9$ **c.** 25×9 **d.** $9 + 25$

Division and remainders

Farmer Jones' hen has laid 13 eggs.

He puts the eggs into cartons. Each carton holds 6 eggs.
He fills 2 cartons but there is 1 egg left over.

If his hen laid 20 eggs, how many cartons
would Farmer Jones fill?

How many eggs would be left over?

Numbers that are left over in division are called remainders.

Exercise 2

These eggs are packed in cartons in groups of six.

Find the remainder of eggs left over in these questions.

1. 7 eggs	**2.** 9 eggs	**3.** 15 eggs	**4.** 21 eggs
5. 25 eggs	**6.** 32 eggs	**7.** 19 eggs	**8.** 35 eggs
9. 12 eggs	**10.** 29 eggs	**11.** 43 eggs	**12.** 23 eggs

Exercise 3

These cakes are packed in their boxes in
groups of 5.

If the baker makes 12 cakes, how many boxes will
he use?
How many cakes will be left over?

He will use two boxes and 2 cakes will be left over.

Write down   **a.** the number of boxes used
              b. the number of cakes left over
for each of these questions. Write your answers on a table as shown.

	No. of cakes	Boxes	Remainder
1.	11	2	1
2.			
3.			

1. 11 cakes	**2.** 16 cakes	**3.** 8 cakes	**4.** 13 cakes
5. 18 cakes	**6.** 19 cakes	**7.** 22 cakes	**8.** 33 cakes
9. 40 cakes	**10.** 47 cakes	**11.** 56 cakes	**12.** 64 cakes

Exercise 4

The baker now uses boxes that hold 8 cakes each.

Write down   **a.** the number of boxes used
              b. the number of the remainder
for each question. Write your answer on a table as before.

1. 9 cakes	**2.** 12 cakes	**3.** 15 cakes	**4.** 17 cakes
5. 20 cakes	**6.** 27 cakes	**7.** 42 cakes	**8.** 36 cakes
9. 55 cakes	**10.** 48 cakes	**11.** 63 cakes	**12.** 73 cakes

Multiplying by 10

■ Use this square as a unit

Use this strip as a ten

Use this block as a hundred

Exercise 5

Copy these drawings.
Write the number represented by the shapes.
The first one is done for you.

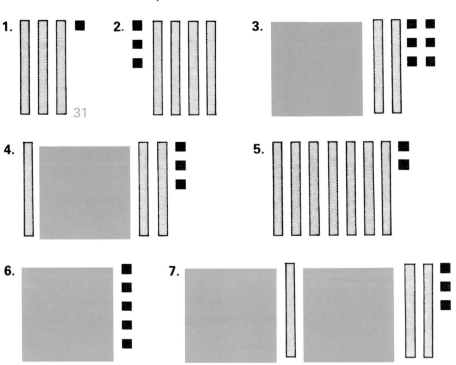

1. 31

Exercise 6

Use drawings like the ones above to show these numbers.

1. 27   **2.** 74

3. 35   **4.** 309

5. 3×2 **6.** 4×2

7. 3×3 **8.** 2×5

You could draw the answer to question 8 in two different ways. It is easier to draw 1 ten than 10 units.

either **a.**   or **b.**

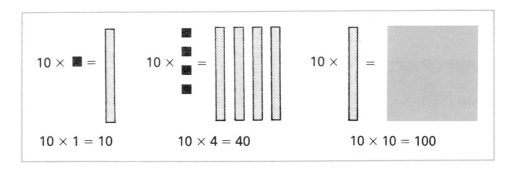

$10 \times 1 = 10$ $10 \times 4 = 40$ $10 \times 10 = 100$

Exercise 7   Draw the numbers which are 10 times bigger than these.

1. 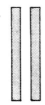   **2.** ■ ■ ■   **3.** ■ ■ ■ ■ ■ ■ ■

4.   **5.** 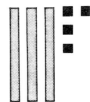   **6.**

7.   **8.**    **9.**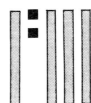

10. Now write out in your book a multiplication statement for
each of the drawings above,
like this: $10 \times 2 = 20$

Look at your answers to question 10.
There is a pattern in the answers. $10 \times 2 = 20$
$10 \times 7 = 70$
$10 \times 11 = 110$

When a number is multiplied by 10, you can see that
the units move to the tens column,
the tens move to the hundreds column, and so on.
We put a nought at the end of the number.

Exercise 8   Multiply these numbers by 10.

1. 9	**2.** 12	**3.** 15	**4.** 19	**5.** 20	**6.** 21
7. 27	**8.** 30	**9.** 35	**10.** 39	**11.** 41	**12.** 63

Number patterns

Tables Practice

Exercise 1

Write down the answers to these problems.

1. $6 \times 2 = *$ **2.** $2 \times 6 = *$ **3.** $5 \times 4 = *$

4. $2 \times 7 = *$ **5.** $8 \times 3 = *$ **6.** $3 \times 4 = *$

7. $8 \times 10 = *$ **8.** $7 \times 5 = *$ **9.** $7 \times 3 = *$

10. $3 \times 9 = *$ **11.** $10 \times 5 = *$ **12.** $6 \times 9 = *$

This is a multiplication table for numbers 1 to 10.

It can be used to answer problems like those in Exercise 1.

$3 \times 4 = 12$

$4 \times 9 = 36$

X	1	2	3	4	5	6	7	8	9	10
1	1	2	3	4	5	6	7	8	9	10
2	2	4	6	8	10	12	14	16	18	20
3	3	6	9	12	15	18	21	24	27	30
4	4	8	12	16	20	24	28	32	36	40
5	5	10	15	20	25	30	35	40	45	50
6	6	12	18	24	30	36	42	48	54	60
7	7	14	21	28	35	42	49	56	63	70
8	8	16	24	32	40	48	56	64	72	80
9	9	18	27	36	45	54	63	72	81	90
10	10	20	30	40	50	60	70	80	90	100

Exercise 2

Use the table above to help you to answer these questions.

1. $9 \times 7 = *$ **2.** $8 \times 8 = *$ **3.** $5 \times 9 = *$

4. $8 \times 7 = *$ **5.** $10 \times 9 = *$ **6.** $7 \times 7 = *$

7. $6 \times 10 = *$ **8.** $8 \times 9 = *$ **9.** $5 \times 8 = *$

10. $9 \times 9 = *$ **11.** $10 \times 10 = *$ **12.** $7 \times 8 = *$

Exercise 3

Copy these statements.
Use the table to say whether they are true or false.

1. $4 \times 5 = 5 \times 4$ **2.** $7 \times 6 = 6 \times 7$ **3.** $4 \times 4 = 2 \times 8$

4. $3 \times 9 = 7 \times 4$ **5.** $2 \times 2 \times 5 = 2 \times 10$ **6.** $4 \times 2 \times 5 = 2 \times 3 \times 7$

Factors

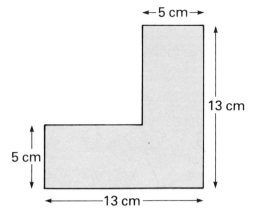

Cut a shape like this
from a piece of card

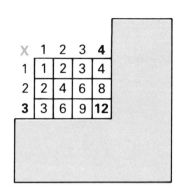

Put this shape over the
multiplication table (page 76) like this.

The number in the corner is 12
so, 12 = 3 × 4.

Here are three other ways of getting 12

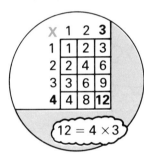

12 = 4 × 3

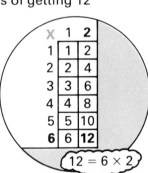

12 = 6 × 2

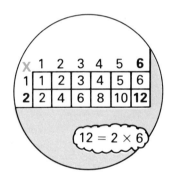

12 = 2 × 6

We say that (3,4) (4,3) (6,2) (2,6) are factor pairs of 12.
There are two more factor pairs, (1,12) and (12,1).

Exercise 4

What factor pairs are used to make up these numbers?

1.
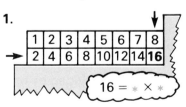

16 = * × *

2.
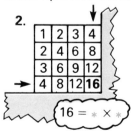

16 = * × *

3.
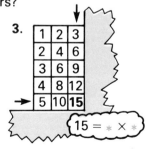

15 = * × *

Exercise 5

1. Find four factor pairs for 10.   2. Find some factor pairs for 15.

3. Find some factor pairs for 21.   4. Find some factor pairs for 8.

5. Find some factor pairs for each of the following numbers:
   a. 24   b. 9   c. 25   d. 36   e. 16   f. 40

Factor trees

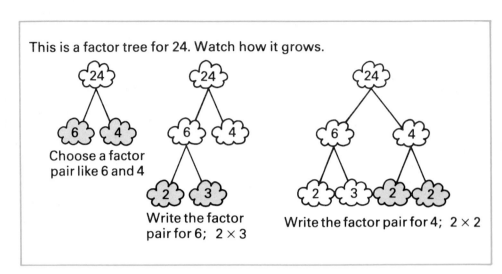

This is a factor tree for 24. Watch how it grows.

Choose a factor pair like 6 and 4

Write the factor pair for 6; 2 × 3

Write the factor pair for 4; 2 × 2

Copy and complete these factor trees.

1.   2.   3.  4.   5.

6.    7.   8. 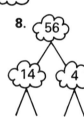   9.    10.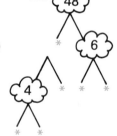

This is the last line of the factor tree for 24.
The tree stops here because these numbers can only be divided by one or themselves. If the tree was continued, it would go on for ever.

Copy and complete these factor trees as far as you can.

1.   2.   3.   4.   5.   6.

The numbers 4, 8, 12, 16, 20, 24, . . . are all in the 4 times table.

We say that these numbers are all divisible by 4. This means that 4 divides into these numbers without leaving a remainder.

Notice that 6 for example does not appear in the 4 times table.
This is because 6 is not divisible by 4; $6 \div 4$ is 1 with a remainder of 2.

X	1	2	3	4	5	6	7	8	9	10
1	1	2	3	4	5	6	7	8	9	10
2	2	4	6	8	10	12	14	16	18	20
3	3	6	9	12	15	18	21	24	27	30
4	4	8	12	16	20	24	28	32	36	40
5	5	10	15	20	25	30	35	40	45	50
6	6	12	18	24	30	36	42	48	54	60
7	7	14	21	28	35	42	49	56	63	70
8	8	16	24	32	40	48	56	64	72	80
9	9	18	27	36	45	54	63	72	81	90
10	10	20	30	40	50	60	70	80	90	100

Exercise 8

Copy the part of the multiplication table shown below.
Three extra boxes have been added to each table. Fill in the extra boxes.

		8	9	10			
1	...	8	9	10			
2	...	16	18	20			
3	...	24	27	30			
4	...	32	36	40	44	48	52
5	...	40	45	50			
6	...	48	54	60			
7	...	56	63	70			
8	...	64	72	80			
9	...	72	81	90			
10	...	80	90	100			

Exercise 9

Answer these questions.

1. Is 22 divisible by 2?   2. Is 45 divisible by 9?

3. Is 63 divisible by 7?   4. Is 57 divisible by 7?

5. Is 42 divisible by 5?   6. Is 27 divisible by 2?

7. Is 60 divisible by 5?   8. Is 96 divisible by 8?

9. Is 78 divisible by 7?   10. Is 25 divisible by 3?

11. Is 117 divisible by 9?   12. Is 39 divisible by 3?

Prime numbers

There are 10 pupils in class 2T. They each have their own desk.
Here are their ten desks.

The desks could be arranged like this:

2 rows of 5 desks

Draw three more ways of arranging these desks in equal rows or columns.

Exercise 10

Draw three different ways of arranging these desks in equal rows or columns

1. 10 desks   2. 18 desks

3. 15 desks   4. 20 desks

If there are 5 desks you could only arrange them in two ways:

1 row of 5 desks

or   5 rows of 1 desk

There are only 2 ways of arranging the desks because 5 is only divisible by 1 and itself.

5 has only one factor pair (1,5)

A number which is only divisible by 1 and itself is called a prime number.

Exercise 11

In each list of numbers, say which number is the prime number.

1. 4, 6, 3, 9, 12   2. 2, 4, 8, 10, 15   3. 6, 3, 16, 14, 4

4. 4, 8, 10, 7, 9   5. 8, 6, 9, 12, 11   6. 13, 15, 20, 25, 30

Square numbers

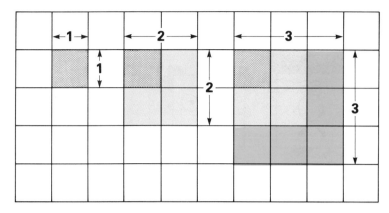

The 1st square number is 1. It is 1 square across and 1 square down.
$1 \times 1 = 1$

The 2nd square number is 4. It is 2 squares across and 2 squares down.
$2 \times 2 = 4$

The 3rd square number is 9. It is 3 squares across and 3 squares down.
$3 \times 3 = 9$

Exercise 12

Draw the next three square numbers on squared paper. Write a sentence under each drawing like the sentences above.

Exercise 13

Use the times table below to help you with this exercise.

X	1	2	3	4	5	6	7	8	9	10
1	1	2	3	4	5	6	7	8	9	10
2	2	4	6	8	10	12	14	16	18	20
3	3	6	9	12	15	18	21	24	27	30
4	4	8	12	16	20	24	28	32	36	40
5	5	10	15	20	25	30	35	40	45	50
6	6	12	18	24	30	36	42	48	54	60
7	7	14	21	28	35	42	49	56	63	70
8	8	16	24	32	40	48	56	64	72	80
9	9	18	27	36	45	54	63	72	81	90
10	10	20	30	40	50	60	70	80	90	100

The shaded boxes show the first 3 square numbers.

1. Make a list of all the square numbers from 1 to 100.

2. Work out the next two square numbers after 100.

Review 3

A. Shape

One of these dolls contains diamonds. Use the clues below to decide which one.

a.	b.	c.	d.	e.	f.

The diamond-filled doll has a round nose.
The diamond-filled doll has a square head.
The diamond-filled doll has a rectangular mouth.
The diamond-filled doll has triangles on its tie. Which doll is it?

B. Graphs

This graph shows the temperature during the course of one day, between 9 o'clock in the morning and 6 o'clock in the evening.

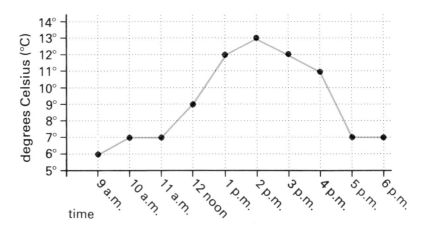

1. What was the temperature at 12 noon?

2. What was the temperature at 4 p.m.?

3. What was the temperature at 9 a.m.?

4. At what time did the temperature reach 13°C?

5. On two occasions the temperature reached 12°C. At what times did this occur?

6. How many degrees did the temperature drop between:
   a. 2 p.m. and 3 p.m.?   **b.** 3 p.m. and 4 p.m.?   **c.** 4 p.m. and 5 p.m.?

C. Fractions

1. If you gave away half of the eight chocolates in the box, how many would you have left?

2. How many chocolates are there in a quarter of the box?

3. One half of the chocolates is the same as ____ quarters or $\frac{1}{2} = \frac{*}{4}$

4. Copy and complete each pair of equivalent fractions.

a.

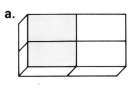

$\frac{1}{2} = \frac{*}{4}$

b.

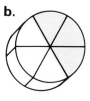

$\frac{1}{2} = \frac{*}{6}$

c.

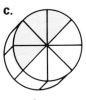

$\frac{1}{2} = \frac{*}{8}$

d.

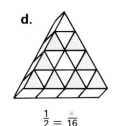

$\frac{1}{2} = \frac{*}{16}$

D. Position

Look at the map. Imagine you are standing at x facing the railway bridge.

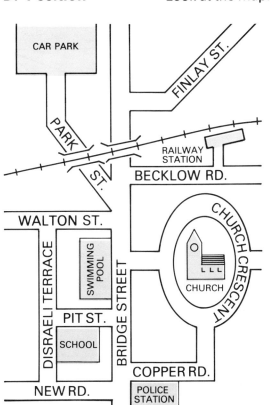

X You are standing here facing the railway bridge.

1. What is the first road on the left?

2. How many turnings on the right is Finlay St.?

3. There are two bridges on the map. In which streets are the bridges?

4. Which is the second street on the left?

5. The school is found at the junction of two roads; which roads are they?

6. Write down the directions to the railway station.

7. Write down the directions to the car park.

8. Imagine that you are standing at the car park. Write down the directions to the church.

9. Imagine that you are standing by the school in Disraeli Terrace. Write down the directions to the car park going by Pit St.

10. Imagine that you are standing by the Police Station in Copper Rd. Write down the directions to Walton St. by going along Pit St.

E. Triangles

1. Copy out these three sentences and fill in the missing words.

   a. The sides of an equilateral triangle are all the ____ length.

   b. An isosceles triangle has ____ sides of the same length.

   c. The three sides of a scalene triangle are all ____ .

2. Copy and complete the table below. Say whether the triangles are scalene, isosceles or equilateral.

Triangle	Type
a	equilateral

a.

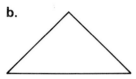

b.

c.

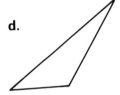

d.

e.

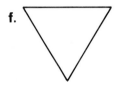

f.

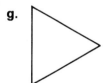

g.

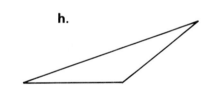

h.

3. Use a ruler and a pair of compasses to construct these triangles.

   a. 4 cm, 5 cm, 3 cm   b. 5·5 cm, 4·5 cm, 7·5 cm

   c. 3·6 cm, 4·7 cm, 6·1 cm

F. Codes

A	B	C	D	E	F	G	H	J
20	6	11	16	22	30	8	17	5

J	K	L	M	N	O	P	Q
46	4	12	27	15	9	14	24

R	S	T	U	V	W	X	Y	Z
40	7	13	4	2	23	29	10	19

Use the information above to put these messages into code.
Code each letter like this: A (2 × 10) or A (16 + 4) or A (5 × 4), etc.

a. MATHS IS FUN   b. I LIKE TEACHERS

G. Coordinates

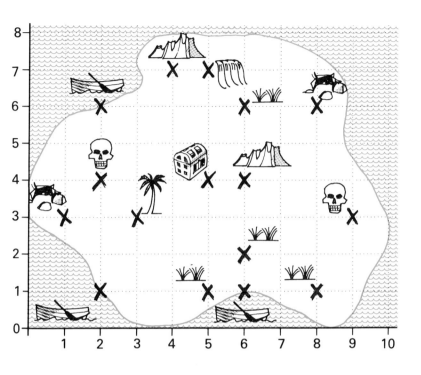

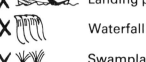 Key to the map of Treasure Island

 Landing point

 Waterfall

Swamplands

Grave

 Woodland

 Mountains

 Buried Treasure

 Cave

Answer these questions about the map. Use the key to the right to help you.

1. Where are the three landing points?

2. What can be found at (3,3)?

3. Where would you go to drink fresh water?

4. What are the positions of the four swamps?

5. What will you see at (4,7) and (6,4)?

6. How many graves are there on the island?

7. What are the positions of the graves?

8. Where will you find the two caves?

9. Write down the coordinates of four places in the sea.

10. Where could you find buried treasure?

H. Time

Match the time on each digital clock with the correct clock time.

1.   2.   3.  4.  5.

a. `18 : 20`   b. `2 : 48`   c. `7 : 55`   d. `16 : 05`   e. `18 : 39`

The Youth Club

Exercise 1   Here is a bar chart showing attendances at the Youth Club for one week.

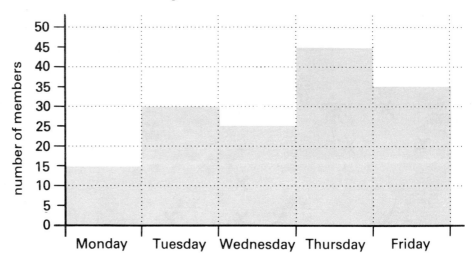

1. How many members attended   **a.** on Monday   **b.** on Tuesday
                                 c. on Wednesday **d.** on Thursday
                                 e. on Friday?

2. Each member pays 10p to attend.
   How much money was collected   **a.** on Monday   **b.** on Tuesday
                                    c. on Wednesday **d.** on Thursday
                                    e. on Friday?

3. How much money was collected during the week altogether?

Exercise 2

The Youth Club are designing a new membership card.
The card must have the following things written on it.

    Warren View Youth Club   Name

    Membership number   Address

Draw a rectangle the same size as the one here.

Design a new membership card.

Decorate it with patterns and geometric shapes.

Membership card.

6 cm

7 cm

The Youth Club competition

It is competition night at the Youth Club.
There are four events in the competition: table tennis
                                            darts
                                            cards
                                            snooker

Six people take part in the competition.

Here is how they did in the four events.

Table tennis	Darts	Cards	Snooker
1st Mary	1st Sally	1st Leroy	1st Leroy
2nd Carlos	2nd Mary	2nd Jan	2nd Sally
3rd Sally	3rd Carlos	3rd Sally	3rd Carlos
4th Leroy	4th Leroy	4th Mary	4th Sam
5th Jan	5th Sam	5th Carlos	5th Mary
6th Sam	6th Jan	6th Sam	6th Jan

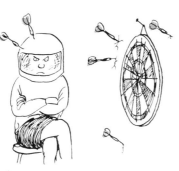

Here is the points table

1st	= 8 points
2nd	= 7 points
3rd	= 5 points
4th	= 3 points
5th	= 2 points
6th	= 1 point

Exercise 3

Copy the results table shown below.

Write on your copy the total score and the position of each competitor.

Name	Total score	Position
Jan		
Leroy		
Mary		
Sally		
Sam		
Carlos		

The Youth Club canteen

This is Mrs. Bright. She runs the Youth Club canteen.

Here is the canteen price list.

Tea	14p
Coffee	20p
Cola	32p
Biscuits	12p
Chews	4p
Crisps	15p
Roll	25p

Exercise 4

How much have these members spent in the canteen?

1. Sally bought a cup of coffee and a bag of crisps.

2. Leroy bought a can of cola and two biscuits.

3. Mary bought a cup of tea, a bag of crisps and a chew.

4. Tom bought two cups of tea and a roll.

5. Jan bought two cans of cola and two bags of crisps.

Profits

6. If the Youth Club make 4p profit on every bag of crisps sold, how much profit would they make on **a.** 6 bags **b.** 10 bags **c.** 12 bags?

7. If the Youth Club make 7p profit on every can of cola sold, how much profit would they make on **a.** 4 cans **b.** 10 cans **c.** 8 cans?

8. If the Youth Club make 5p profit on every biscuit sold, how much profit would they make on **a.** 7 biscuits **b.** 10 biscuits **c.** 12 biscuits?

Exercise 5

Mrs. Bright keeps a cash book.

In her cash book she writes down each night how much money she takes (income).

She also writes down on the day the money that she spends (expenses).

A page from her cash book is shown on the right.

1. Copy the page of her cash book neatly and complete it.

2. What was the total income for the week?

3. What were the total expenses for the week?

4. What was the total profit (income *minus* expenses)?

	Income	Expenses
Mon.	£4·45	£5·28
Tue.	£6·22	—
Wed.	£3·10	£0·56
Thurs.	£10·03	£0·60
Fri.	£12·25	—

Youth Club fund raising

Exercise 6

The Youth Club needs a new minibus.
To raise the money, the members decide to organise a sponsored swim.

Here are the sponsorship forms of three club members.

Name __Bob__

Lengths completed __6__

Sponsor	Amount per length	Total
Mr. King	2p	12p
Mrs. Smith	3p	*
Mary	2p	*
Billy	1p	*
Mrs. Ellis	3p	*

Name __Anne__

Lengths completed __10__

Sponsor	Amount per length	Total
Mrs. Roper	3p	*
Mrs. Allen	6p	*
S. Brown	2p	*
Tom	2p	*
Mr. Greg	5p	*
Charly	3p	*
Miss Goode	2p	*

Name __Jim__

Lengths completed __9__

Sponsor	Amount per length	Total
Joe	5p	*
Miss Wallis	2p	*
Mr. Crow	3p	*
Mrs. Crow	3p	*
Dean	2p	*
B. Carr	4p	*
S. Carr	3p	*

Copy and complete each form.

1. How much money did Bob raise?

2. How much money did Anne raise?

3. How much money did Jim raise?

4. How much did the three of them raise together?

Exercise 7

Here is another sponsorship form. Copy and complete it.

Name __Jenny__

Lengths completed __8__

Sponsor	Amount per length	Total
B. Brown	4p	*
S. Smith	*	16p
Gill	*	32p
Mr. Khan	3p	*
Mrs. Khan	*	40p
Miss Clegg	*	80p
	TOTAL	___

The Youth Club journey

Exercise 8

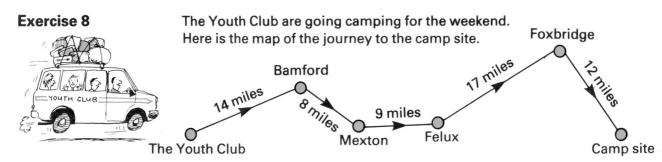

The Youth Club are going camping for the weekend. Here is the map of the journey to the camp site.

1. How many miles is the journey from the club to the camp site?

2. If the minibus travels 30 miles in one hour, how long will the journey take?

3. If the minibus travels 5 miles on a litre of petrol, how many litres will the minibus use on the journey?

Exercise 9

During the weekend, the party go walking. They divide into two groups, A and B. Below is a map of the routes the two groups take.

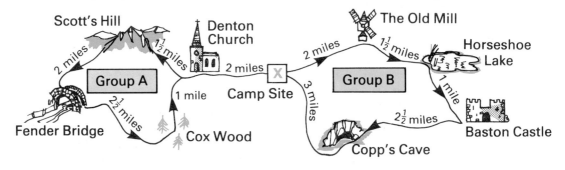

1. How far is it to walk from the camp site to:
   a. Horseshoe Lake   b. Scott's Hill   c. Fender Bridge?

2. How far does Group A walk?   3. How far does Group B walk?

Exercise 10

The cost of staying at the camp site is 25p a night for each person. To park the minibus costs 60p a night.
There are 11 members camping for two nights.

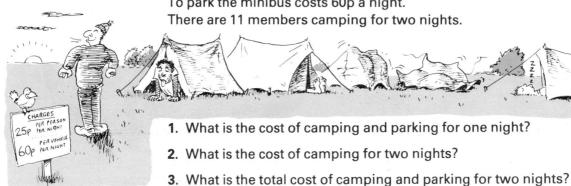

1. What is the cost of camping and parking for one night?

2. What is the cost of camping for two nights?

3. What is the total cost of camping and parking for two nights?

Section 16 **Area**

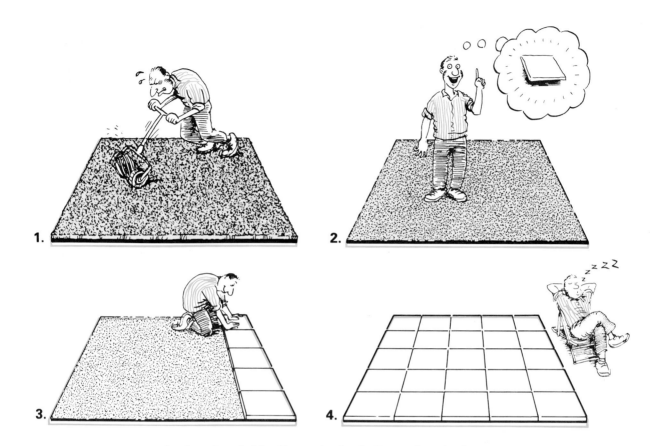

In drawing 1, Mr. Green is tired of mowing the lawn.
In drawing 2, he decides to cover the lawn with square slabs.
In drawing 3, Mr. Green lays a row of 5 square slabs.
In drawing 4, he has laid five rows of slabs altogether.

How many square slabs did it take to cover the whole of the lawn?

We say that the area of the lawn is 25 squares.

Exercise 1   Mr. Green lays slabs for his neighbours' gardens. Count the squares and
find the area of each lawn.

1.

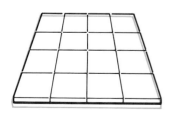

Mr. Brown's lawn has an area
of ____ squares.

2.

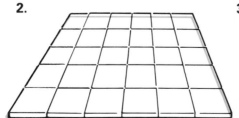

Mr. Black's lawn has an area
of ____ squares.

3.

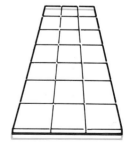

Miss White's lawn has an area
of ____ squares.

Exercise 2

Mr. Green is paving each lawn outlined in green. He has marked where the slabs will be placed. Find the area of each lawn.

1. The lawn has an area of _____ squares.

2. The lawn has an area of _____ squares.

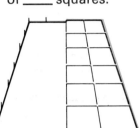

3. The lawn has an area of _____ squares

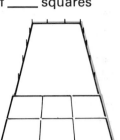

4. The lawn has an area of _____ squares.

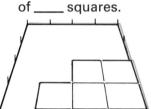

5. The lawn has an area of _____ squares.

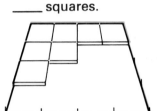

6. The lawn has an area of _____ squares.

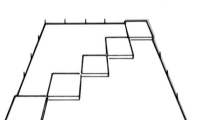

7. The lawn has an area of _____ squares.

8. The lawn has an area of _____ squares.

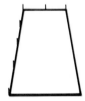

9. The lawn has an area of _____ squares.

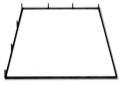

Exercise 3

Copy and complete each sentence below.

1. The garden has an area of _____ squares.

2. This garden has an area of _____ squares.

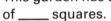
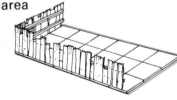

3. This garden has an area of _____ squares.

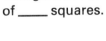

4. The playground has an area of _____ squares.

To find the area of a rectangle or a square, you do not need to count squares on a grid.
In this rectangle, there are 2 rows with 5 squares in each row.
The area of the rectangle $= 2 \times 5$ squares
$$= 10 \text{ squares}$$

In this square, there are 3 rows with 3 squares in each row.
The area of the square $= 3 \times 3$ squares
$$= 9 \text{ squares}$$

Exercise 4

Copy and complete these two sentences for each drawing below.
a. The area = _____ × _____ squares.
b. The area = _____ squares.

1.

2.

3.

4.

5.

6.

7.

8.

9.

10.

11.

12.

13.

14.

15.

page 93

The unit used to measure area is the square.
We use squares that are a standard size. This is a square whose sides are all 1 cm long. It is called a centimetre-square (written 1 cm²).
We would use this square to find the area of small surfaces like the cover of a book.

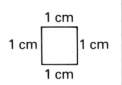

Exercise 5

Complete these two statements for each drawing below:
a. Area = ＿＿ cm × ＿＿ cm.

b. Area = ＿＿ centimetre-squares or ＿＿ cm².
The drawings are *not* full size.

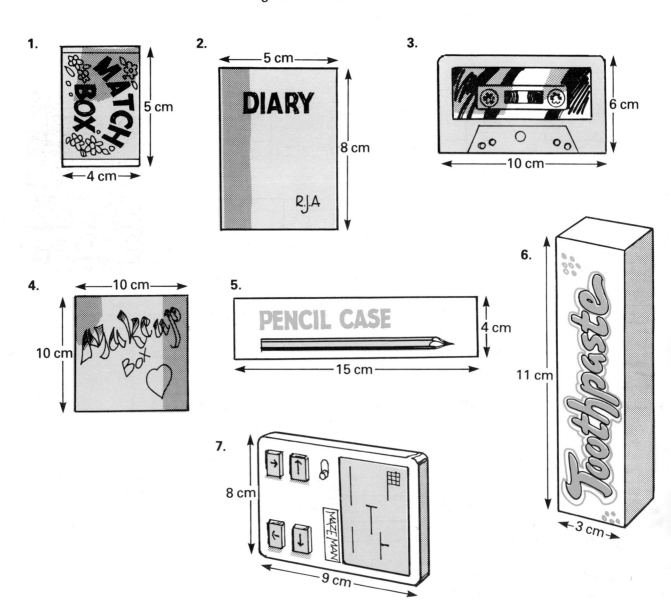

For measuring large areas, we use a bigger square. We use the metre-square (written m^2). The sides of the square are all 1 m long. It is too big to draw full size.

1 m

1 m   1 m

1 m

(not full size)

Exercise 6

Complete these two statements for each drawing below:

a. Area = ____ m × ____ m.

b. Area = ____ metre-squares or ____ m^2.
The drawings are *not* full size.

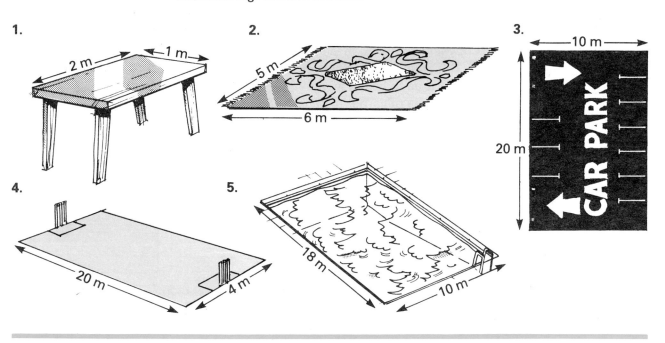

1. 2 m   1 m

2. 5 m   6 m

3. 10 m   20 m   CAR PARK

4. 20 m   4 m

5. 18 m   10 m

Exercise 7

Find the missing length in each of the drawings below.

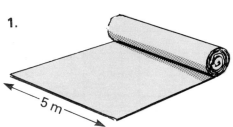

1. 5 m

The area of the carpet is 50 m^2.
If its width is 5 m, what is its length?

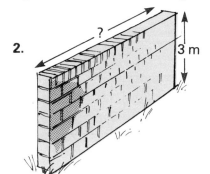

2. ?   3 m

The area of the wall is 33 m^2.
If its height is 3 m, what is its length?

To cover the floor of this room with a carpet, we would need to buy a carpet 6 m by 6 m, then cut away the corner piece, 2 m × 2 m.

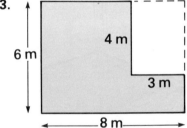

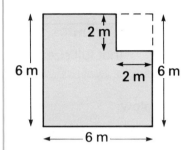

This is a plan of the carpet. The dotted line shows the piece to be cut away.

The area of the whole carpet = 6 m × 6 m
$\qquad\qquad\qquad\qquad\qquad$ = 36 m²

The area to be cut away = 2 m × 2 m
$\qquad\qquad\qquad\qquad$ = 4 m²

So the area of carpet to be laid down = 36 m² − 4 m²
$\qquad\qquad\qquad\qquad\qquad\qquad\qquad$ = 32 m²

Exercise 8

Copy and complete these three statements for each drawing.
a. The area of the whole carpet = _____ m²
b. The area to be cut away = _____ m²
c. The area of carpet to be laid down = _____ m²

The drawings are not full size.

1.
2 m
2 m
6 m
6 m

2.
3 m
5 m
2 m
6 m

3.
4 m
6 m
3 m
8 m

4.
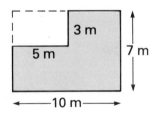
3 m
5 m
7 m
10 m

5.
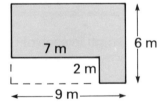
7 m
2 m
6 m
9 m

6.
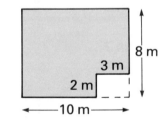
3 m
2 m
8 m
10 m

7.
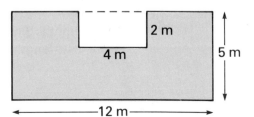
2 m
4 m
5 m
12 m

8.
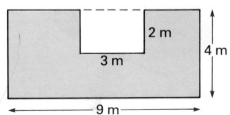
2 m
3 m
4 m
9 m

The area of the whole square = 4 × 4 squares
                              = 16 squares.

The square has been cut into two halves. Each half is
a triangle.

The area of each triangle is half the area of the
square, or 16 squares ÷ 2
                Area of triangle = 8 squares.

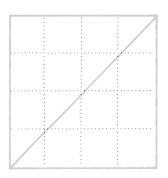

Exercise 9

Find the area of these triangles. Copy and complete these two statements.
a. The area of the rectangle = _____ cm².
b. The area of the triangle = _____ cm².

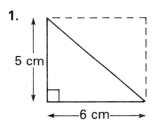 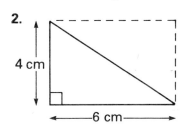 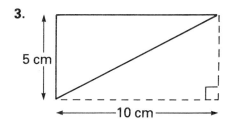

1. 5 cm, 6 cm

2. 4 cm, 6 cm

3. 5 cm, 10 cm

Exercise 10

Find the area of these triangles using the same method.

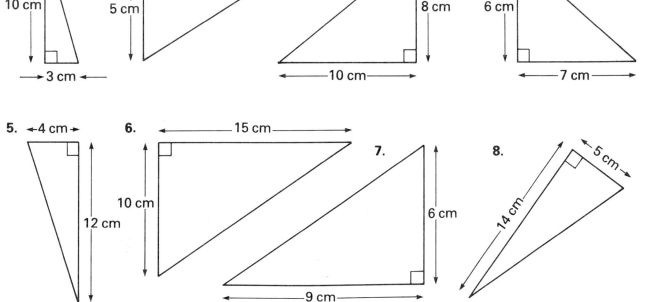

1. 10 cm, 3 cm

2. 8 cm, 5 cm

3. 8 cm, 10 cm

4. 6 cm, 7 cm

5. 4 cm, 12 cm

6. 15 cm, 10 cm

7. 6 cm, 9 cm

8. 5 cm, 14 cm

Shape

Exercise 1   Find the radius of each of these objects.

1. The radius of the tyre is _____ cm.   **2.** The radius of the dial is _____ cm.

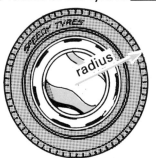   

3. The radius of the stone in the ring is _____ cm.   **4.** The radius of the plug is _____ cm.

Exercise 2   Copy and complete the sentences below.
The questions are about the drawings above.

1. The diameter of the plug is ___cm.   **2.** The diameter of the tyre is ___ cm.

3. The diameter of the dial is ___cm.   **4.** The diameter of the stone is___ cm.

Exercise 3   Copy and complete the table below.

radius	diameter
5 cm	*
$2\frac{1}{2}$ cm	*
7 cm	*
*	20 cm
*	30 cm
16 cm	*
*	50 cm
$4\frac{1}{2}$ cm	*
$10\frac{1}{2}$ cm	*

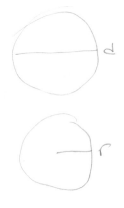

$2r = d$

Lines and circles

The centre of each circle is marked O.

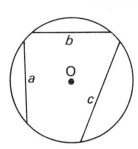

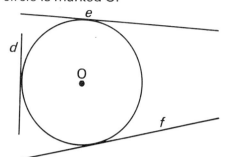

The lines marked *a, b* and *c* are called chords.

Chords touch the circle in two places. Chords do not go through the centre of the circle.

The lines marked *d, e* and *f* are called tangents.

Tangents touch the circle in only one place.

Exercise 4

Copy and complete the sentences below.

1. The centre of the circle is marked with the letter _____

2. The line marked *r* is the _____ of the circle.

3. Lines *x* and *y* are called _____

4. The shortest chord is line _____

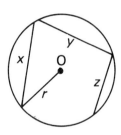

Exercise 5

Copy and complete the sentences below.

1. The line *j* is called the _____

2. The lines *h* and *n* are called _____

3. The line *k* is called a _____

4. The lines *p* and *m* are called _____

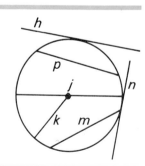

Exercise 6

Measure each line, then copy and complete the sentences below.

1. The radius is _____ cm long.

2. The tangent line is _____ cm long.

3. The shortest chord is _____ cm long.

4. The diameter is _____ cm long.

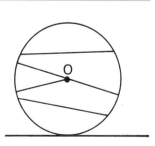

Polygons

Any closed shape with straight sides is a polygon.

We have already used these polygons.

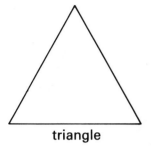 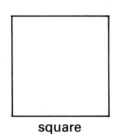 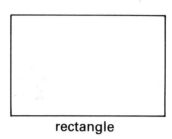 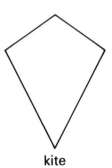

triangle   square   rectangle   kite

The shapes below are called regular polygons.

pentagon
5 sides
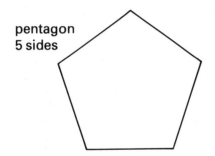

hexagon
6 sides
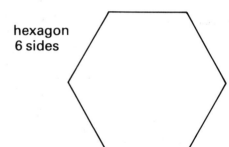

heptagon
7 sides
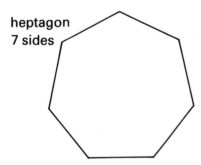

octagon
8 sides
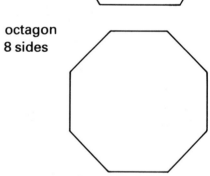

A regular polygon has sides that are all the same length.
A regular polygon has angles that are all the same size.

Exercise 7   Name these polygons.

1. 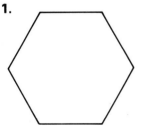   **2.**    **3.** 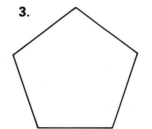   **4.** 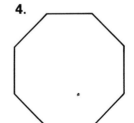   **5.**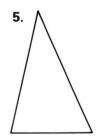

Exercise 8

Put these shapes through the sorter. See where they come out.

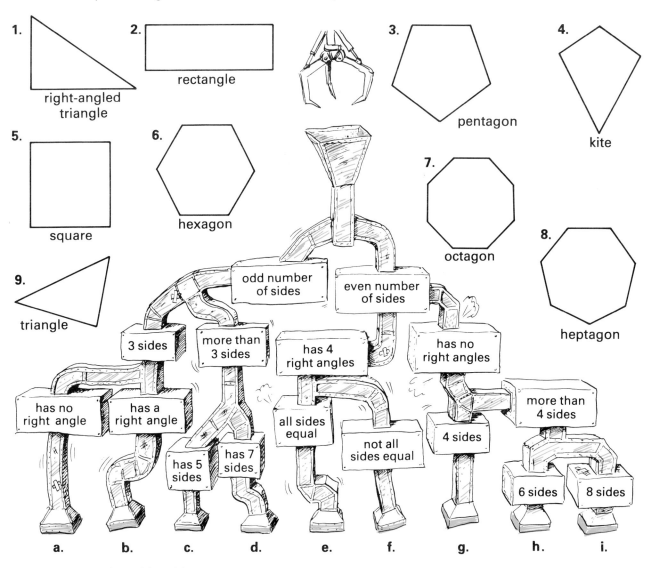

1. right-angled triangle
2. rectangle
3. pentagon
4. kite
5. square
6. hexagon
7. octagon
8. heptagon
9. triangle

Copy and complete this table.

shape number	where does it come out	description			name
1.	b.	odd number of sides	3 sides	has a right angle	right-angled triangle

Symmetry

Turn this page upside down. What do you notice about the word above?
Even when you turn the word upside down, it still looks the same and it
still reads 'chump'.

Exercise 9

Which of the words below look the same when they are turned upside
down?

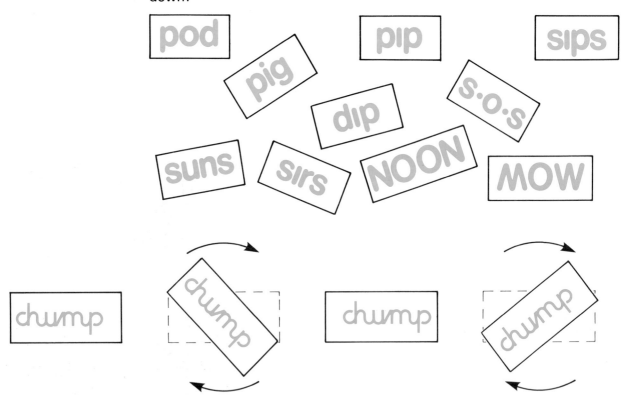

In one whole turn (one rotation) the word chump looks the same twice.
The drawing has a rotational symmetry of order 2.

The shape below looks the same three times (at **b, d,** and **f**) in one rotation.
We say this drawing has a rotational symmetry of order 3.

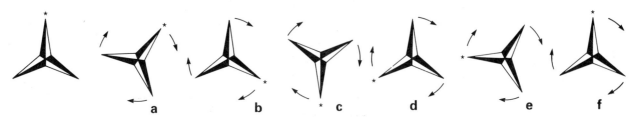

Exercise 10

Copy and complete the table giving the rotational order of the shapes.
It may help if you trace each shape and then turn it round.
Remember, you can only turn the shape through one whole turn.
Put a mark on the shape so you can see when you have completed one turn.

shape	rotational order
a	2
b	
c	1
d	
e	
f	
g	
h	
i	
j	
k	
l	
m	4
n	
p	
q	
r	
s	
t	
u	

a.

b.

c.

d.

e.

f.

g.

h.

i.

j.

k.

l.

m.

n.

p.

q.

r.

s.

t.

u.

We use symbols to represent information, ideas, and also numbers.

This symbol represents one pound in money. Where would you see it?

This symbol represents poison. Where would you see it?

This symbol represents ladies. Where would you see it?

Exercise 1

Each symbol below gives some information.
Write down the meaning of each and where you might find it.

1.    **2.**    **3.**

4.    **5.** "999"   **6.**

7.    **8.**    **9.**

Exercise 2

Make up your own symbols to represent these ideas.

1. No shouting   **2.** This is a classroom   **3.** No teachers allowed

4. Dining room   **5.** Your own name   **6.** Fairground

Dealing with symbols

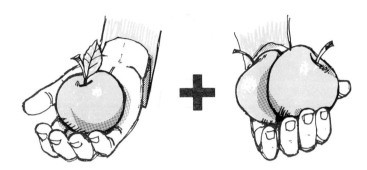

In algebra, we often use symbols to represent objects or numbers. We need to know how to deal with symbols in maths.

In one hand, there is one apple. In the other, there are two apples. Altogether there are 3 apples.
If we choose to use the symbol a for apple, the sum can be written like this: $a + 2a = 3a$

The symbol a was chosen because the word apple starts with a; but we could use any symbol we like.

Exercise 3

Write out a sum for each box and give the answer. Use symbols not words. Look at the example.

Use b for apple.

$2b + 4b = 6b$

1.
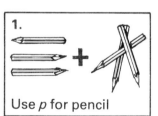
Use p for pencil

2.
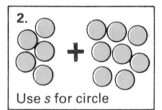
Use s for circle

3.
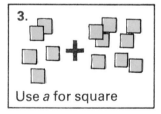
Use a for square

4.
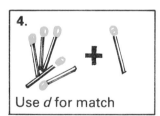
Use d for match

5.
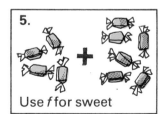
Use f for sweet

6.
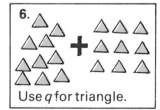
Use q for triangle.

7.
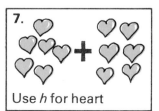
Use h for heart

8.
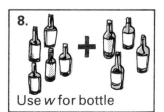
Use w for bottle

9.
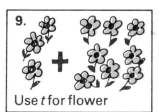
Use t for flower

Exercise 4

Simplify these problems using symbols.
Here is an example:
$5a - 2a = 3a$

1. $6a - 4a =$ **2.** $10p - 8p =$ **3.** $17x - 10x =$

4. $11a - 8a =$ **5.** $12b - 6b =$ **6.** $21e - 10e =$

7. $22d - 5d =$ **8.** $30q - 20q =$ **9.** $32m - 20m =$

10. $50s - 25s =$ **11.** $50x - 28x =$ **12.** $60t - 25t =$

13. $40z - 15z =$ **14.** $34a - 19a =$ **15.** $80n - 25n =$

Exercise 5

Add up these symbols. Be careful to add all of the symbols.
Here is an example:
$a + 2a + 4a = 7a$

1. $b + 5b + 6b =$ **2.** $10a + 3a + 2a =$ **3.** $4s + 3s + 7s =$

4. $9p + 20p + 8p =$ **5.** $14p + 20p + p =$ **6.** $t + 2t + t + 5t =$

7. $a + 5a + 16a =$ **8.** $15x + 5x + 16x =$ **9.** $26a + a + 2a + 3a =$

10. $q + 7q + 10q + q =$ **11.** $2m + 3m + 2m + 10m =$ **12.** $15z + 12z + z + z =$

13. $12a + 10a + a =$ **14.** $15d + 10d + d + 4d =$ **15.** $20x + 17x + 3x =$

Here are 2 apples and 3 bananas.
If we tried to add the two quantities,
we would not say that we had 5 'banapples'.

We can only add symbols that are *alike*.

We can only combine 'a' with 'a' and
'b' with 'b', etc.

a for apple
b for banana
$2a + 3b$ is not $5ab$

Exercise 6

Add up the like symbols in these problems.
Here is an example:
$2a + 3a + 3b + b = 5a + 4b$

1. $a + 2a + 3b =$ **2.** $2a + 5a + 4b + 2b =$ **3.** $6p + 2t + 5p + 4t =$

4. $4s + s + 3r + s =$ **5.** $5q + p + 2p + 6q =$ **6.** $10p + 4q + q + 2q =$

7. $3x + 2y + x + 5y =$ **8.** $10a + 2c + a + 3c =$ **9.** $7f + g + 3g + 3f =$

10. $h + h + 5h + 2j =$ **11.** $2s + 5s + x + s =$ **12.** $4k + 6y + k + 3y =$

13. $5x + x + t + 8t =$ **14.** $4e + 8c + 5e + c =$ **15.** $e + e + t + 9e + t =$

16. $12a + d + 9a + d =$ **17.** $b + 19k + 8k + 9b =$ **18.** $10y + x + 21y + y =$

Balancing problems

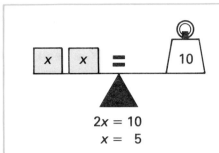

The two sides of the scales balance: they are equal in weight.

We must find out how much each box marked x weighs.

$2x = 10$
$x = 5$

Two x's weigh 10
So one x weighs 5

Exercise 7   Find the weight of the objects marked x.

1.
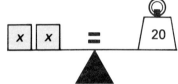

2.
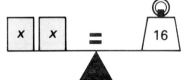

3.
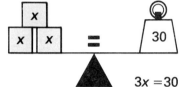

$3x = 30$

4.
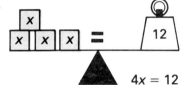

$4x = 12$

5.

6.
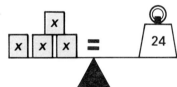

7.
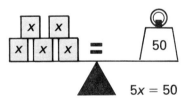

$5x = 50$

8.
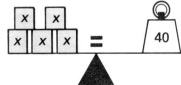

9.
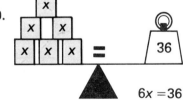

$6x = 36$

10.
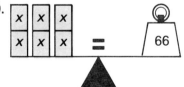

11.
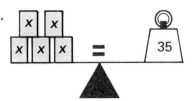

12.
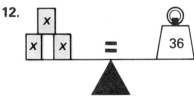

Exercise 8   Find the value or 'weight' of x in these problems.

1. $2x = 20$ **2.** $3x = 30$ **3.** $3x = 6$ **4.** $3x = 15$

5. $2x = 40$ **6.** $3x = 45$ **7.** $5x = 20$ **8.** $5x = 15$

9. $4x = 16$ **10.** $3x = 27$ **11.** $6x = 30$ **12.** $6x = 48$

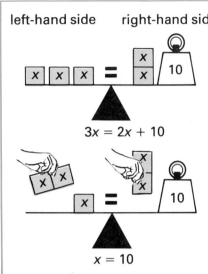

In this problem, there are x's on both sides of the balance.

You need to take $2x$ from the right-hand side.

But the weights must be kept balanced.

So $2x$ must also be taken from the left-hand side.

So x must weigh 10.

left-hand side   right-hand side

$3x = 2x + 10$

$x = 10$

Exercise 9

Find the value or 'weight' of x in each problem.

1.

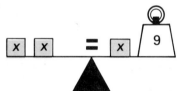

2.

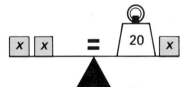

3.

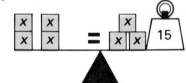

4.

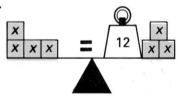

5.

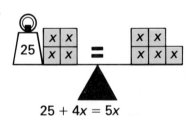

$25 + 4x = 5x$

6.

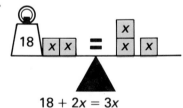

$18 + 2x = 3x$

7.

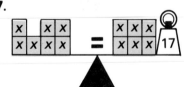

8.

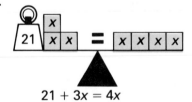

$21 + 3x = 4x$

9.

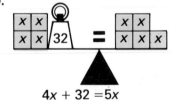

$4x + 32 = 5x$

Exercise 10

Find the value or 'weight' of x in each problem.

1. $3x = 2x + 10$ **2.** $5x = 4x + 12$ **3.** $2x + 6 = 3x$

4. $7x + 1 = 8x$ **5.** $12x + 9 = 13x$ **6.** $25 + 15x = 16x$

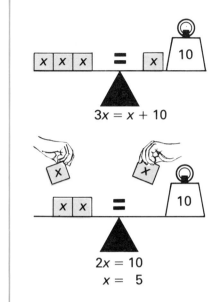

$3x = x + 10$

Here we can take one x from both sides.

We are left with $2x$ only on the left-hand side.

If you need help, look back at page 107.

$2x = 10$
$x = 5$

Exercise 11

Find the value of x in each problem.

1.

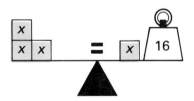

2.

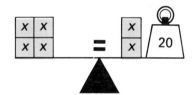

3.

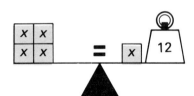

4.

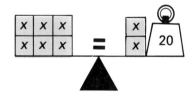

Exercise 12

Find the value of x in each problem.

1. $3x = x + 8$ **2.** $3x = x + 12$ **3.** $4x = 2x + 16$

4. $9x = 7x + 6$ **5.** $5x = 2x + 6$ **6.** $6x = 3x + 15$

7. $7x = 4x + 9$ **8.** $5x = x + 12$ **9.** $10x = 6x + 20$

10. $8x = 4x + 24$ **11.** $9x = 4x + 10$ **12.** $10x = 5x + 30$

13. $10x = 5x + 25$ **14.** $7x = 5x + 2$ **15.** $13x = 7x + 18$

Review 4

A. Shape

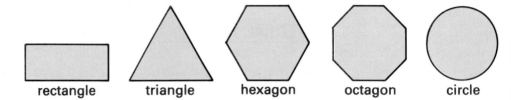

| rectangle | triangle | hexagon | octagon | circle |

Look at each of the three diagrams below. Count how many of each shape. Then copy and complete the table: the first diagram is done for you.

1.

2.

3.

diagram	rectangle	triangle	hexagon	octagon	circle
1	✓	✓✓✓✓	—	—	—
2					
3					

B. Measuring

1. The picture shows four mountains. Use the scale on the left to name them all.

> Mount Snowdon is 1085 m high
>
> Scafell Pike is 978 m high
>
> Ben Nevis is 1343 m high
>
> Carrauntual is 1041 m high

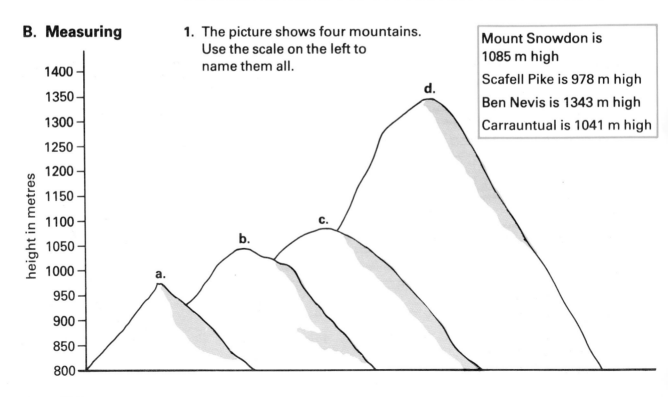

2. Copy and complete the following.

    a. The world's longest tandem bicycle is over 20 _____ long.
               (centimetres – hours – metres – miles)

    b. The world's longest river is the Nile and is 6670 _____ long.
               (millimetres – kilometres – months – centimetres)

    c. A man once ate 144 prunes in 54 _____ to establish a record.
               (days – kilometres – seconds – hours)

    d. The Earth takes about 365 _____ to go once around the Sun.
               (years – months – weeks – days)

    e. A 2p piece is about 2 _____ thick.
               (metres – millimetres – hours – centimetres)

C. Area

1. What is the area of each of these three shapes? Write down your answer in centimetre-squares.

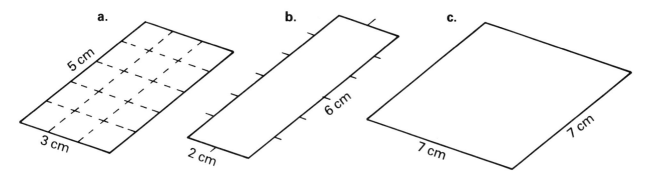

2. Find the area of this hand in cm^2.

Count up all the whole cm squares.

Next add up the 'bits', to an approximate number of whole squares.

Then add up the two numbers of whole squares together.

3. Find the area of your own hand in cm^2.

Place your hand on 1 cm squared grid paper. Draw round your hand.

Count up all the whole cm squares. Then add up the 'bits' to an approximate number of whole squares. Then add the two numbers of whole squares together.

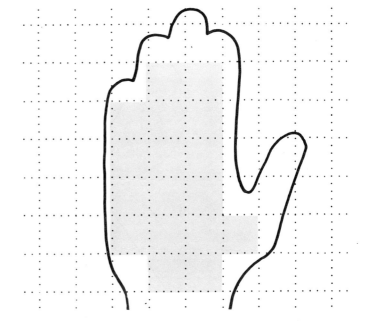

D. Time and distance   The time/distance graph below shows the journey of a coach.

1. How many kilometres did the coach travel in 45 minutes?

2. How far did the coach travel during the first 20 minutes?

3. How long did the coach stop for?

4. How long did the coach take to travel the first 40 kilometres?

5. How far did the coach travel during the last 15 minutes?

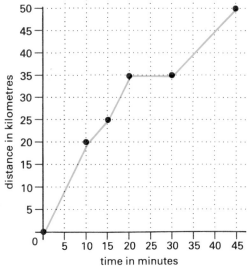

E. Fractions

1. There were 20 people in a room. If half of them left, how many stayed?

2. There are 16 cats and dogs in a house. One quarter of them were dogs. How many cats were there?

3. There were 24 cakes in a shop. If half of them were sold, how many were left?

4. There were 20 cars in a car park. A quarter of them were red. How many red cars were there?

5. Jenny had 30p. She spent half of it. How much had she left?

6. What fraction of each shape is shaded?

a.

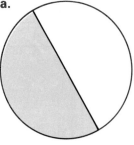

b.

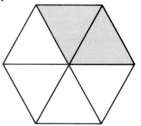

c.

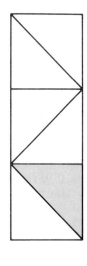

d.

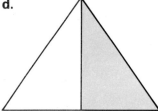

e.

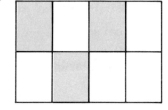

F. Sets

1. Draw three set rings.
   Group the words below into the set rings.
   Give each set a suitable name.

Monday	beef	Wednesday	January
lamb	Sunday	June	August
Friday	pork	July	Saturday

2. **a.** How many people play tennis?
   b. How many people play chess?
   c. How many people play both?

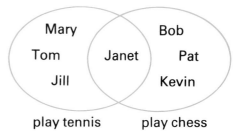

play tennis   play chess

3. **a.** How many people like dancing?
   b. How many people like singing?
   c. How many people like both?

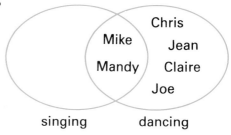

singing   dancing

G. Decimals

Solve these decimal problems.

1. $\begin{array}{r} 3\cdot24 \\ +\ 2\cdot03 \\ \hline \end{array}$
2. $\begin{array}{r} 3\cdot5 \\ +\ 13\cdot6 \\ \hline \end{array}$
3. $\begin{array}{r} 6\cdot51 \\ +0\cdot6 \\ \hline \end{array}$
4. $\begin{array}{r} 21\cdot09 \\ +\ 9\cdot6 \\ \hline \end{array}$
5. $\begin{array}{r} 1\cdot3 \\ 12\cdot6 \\ +\ 9\cdot36 \\ \hline \end{array}$

6. $\begin{array}{r} 9\cdot8 \\ -\ 2\cdot5 \\ \hline \end{array}$
7. $\begin{array}{r} 8\cdot2 \\ -\ 1\cdot0 \\ \hline \end{array}$
8. $\begin{array}{r} 8\cdot2 \\ -\ 5\cdot6 \\ \hline \end{array}$
9. $\begin{array}{r} 16\cdot55 \\ -\ 9\cdot05 \\ \hline \end{array}$
10. $\begin{array}{r} 26\cdot82 \\ -\ 9\cdot6 \\ \hline \end{array}$

11. Put these numbers in order of size, beginning with the smallest number.

    9·3   1·9   2·35   0·88

12. Put these numbers in order of size, beginning with the smallest number.

    23·35   2·86   231·5   6·95

H. Number pattern

Give one factor pair for each number in the factor trees below.

1.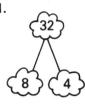

2.

3.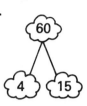

4.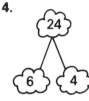

5.

6.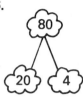

7.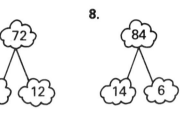

8.

Find three factor pairs for each of these numbers.

9. 28   **10.** 36   **11.** 45   **12.** 50

Find the two prime numbers in each list below.

13. 2, 4, 5, 6, 8   **14.** 3, 7, 10, 15   **15.** 10, 4, 11, 17

16. Copy this list of numbers and underline the 'square numbers'.

1, 3, 4, 5, 7, 9, 12, 16, 20, 25, 28, 30, 42, 44, 49.

I. Algebra

Simplify these expressions. The first one is done for you.

1. $6a + 16a = 22a$ **2.** $2a + 3a + 5a =$ **3.** $7x + 9x + 2x =$

4. $20y + 16y - 8y =$ **5.** $15f + 20f - 9f =$ **6.** $4a + 2b + a + 5b =$

7. $14p + q + q + 3q =$ **8.** $21s + 2s + 3t + 15t =$ **9.** $3n + 5m + 14m + 18n =$

10. Find the value of x in each question.

a. 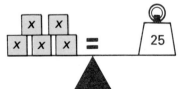   **b.** 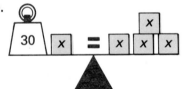   **c.**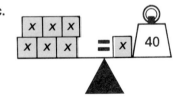

Find the value of the letters in the problems.

11. $2x = 24$ **12.** $5a = 35$ **13.** $3y = 45$

14. $4b = 28$ **15.** $4t = 80$ **16.** $5f = 45$

17. $6p = 54$ **18.** $2x = x + 10$ **19.** $3p = p + 10$

20. $5r = 2r + 18$ **21.** $7t = 3t + 20$ **22.** $6t = 4t + 50$

J. Mixed problems

1. This train is 135 m long.
   How much of the train is still in the tunnel?

   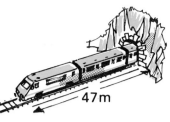

   47m

2. Alice has a paper round. She earns £7 a week.
   How many weeks will she have to work to earn £49?

3. If it is now 10.15, what time will it be in
   25 minutes time?

4. Measure these lines accurately.

5. If you get 25 cans of lemonade in a case, how many cans
   would you get in 6 cases?

6. What is the next number in these number patterns?

   a. 2, 8, 14, 20, ___   **b.** 1, 9, 17, 25, ___   **c.** 5, 12, 19, 26, ___

7. How many 10p pieces are there in £1·30?

8. How many 2p pieces are there in 38p?

9. A piece of string 48 cm long is cut into four equal pieces. How long
   is each piece?

10. Toby buys these items.
    How much did they cost
    altogether?

     27p   18p

    9p

11. How many tiles are covering the following areas?

    a.

    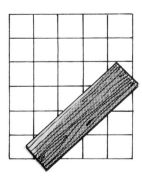

    b.

    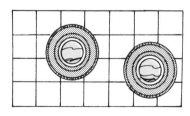

12. This is a counter at a football ground turnstile.   00999
    What will the counter read if one more person goes through the
    turnstile?

Buying a bicycle

Joey tried to save up to buy a new bike.

Joey's newspaper round paid him £9 a week, but
he spent some of this.

Exercise 1

This is Joey's record of his weekly spending and saving.
Copy and complete the table.

week	earnings	spent	saved
1	£9	£3.00	*
2	£9	£2.00	*
3	£9	£5.50	*
4	£9	£1.00	*
5	£9	£0.50	*
6	£9	£0.75	*
7	£9	£3.25	*
8	£9	£2.75	*
9	£9	£4.25	*
10	£9	£1.00	*
		total	*

Exercise 2

Answer these questions using the table above.

1. In which week did Joey spend most of his earnings?

2. In which week did Joey save most of his earnings?

3. In which two weeks did Joey save the same amount of money?

4. How much did Joey save in the first five weeks?

5. How much did Joey save in the last five weeks?

6. How much did Joey earn altogether?

7. How much did Joey save altogether?

8. Joey's father made the amount up to £132. How much money did his
   father give him?

Joey has £132 to spend.
He goes to two bicycle shops and collects their price lists of
racing bikes.

Rapid Bikes Ltd   41 High St.

RACING BIKES SALE

	Normal price	Reduced by
B.R.R. Racer X10	£112	£10
Racer Rapide	£116	£15
Sim's Freewheeler	£130	£8
Super Ace 55	£185	£12
Clubman 99	£158	£23
Champion	£150	£25

Robinson and Sons   151 Church St.

RACER SALE

		Sale price
Super Ace 55	£188	£170
Speed King	£130	£120
Champion	£145	£120
Racer Rapide	£110	£99
Clubman 99	£149	£130
Road Star	£159	£145
B.R.R. Racer X10	£110	£99.50

Exercise 3

1. Make a list of the bikes Joey can afford with £132.

2. Which shop offers the best prices?

3. Joey decides to buy the *Champion* bike.
   a. At which shop would he buy it?
   b. After buying the bike, how much money has he left over?

4. What is the sale price of the *Clubman 99* at Rapid Bikes?

5. What is the sale price of the *Racer Rapide* at Rapid Bikes?

6. What is the sale price of the *Super Ace 55* at Rapid Bikes?

7. How much less is the sale price of the *Speed King* at Robinsons?

8. How much can be saved on the *Racer Rapide* at Robinsons?

After buying his bike, Joey has £12 left. However, he still has to buy several more items for his bike. Here is the list.

One front light.
One back light.
Puncture repair kit.
Padlock and chain.

He goes shopping, and here is a selection of the items he needs.

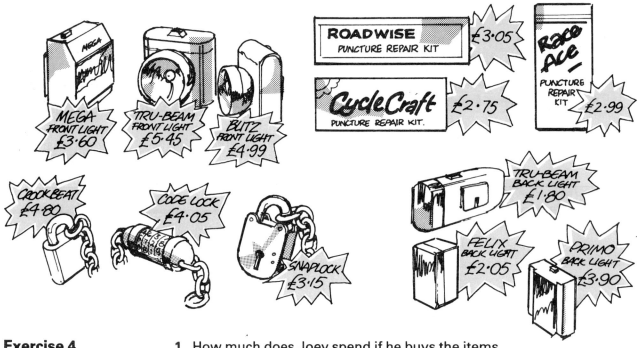

Exercise 4

1. How much does Joey spend if he buys the items he needs at the cheapest prices?

2. How much change from £12 would he have after buying them?

3. If he bought the most expensive front light and back light, how much would he spend?

4. How much is the dearest puncture repair kit?

5. How much is the dearest front light?

6. How much is the cheapest padlock and chain?

7. Which back light costs £2·05?

8. If Joey bought a Tru-Beam front light, and a Code Lock padlock and chain, how much would he spend?

9. If Joey bought a Primo back light and a Road Wise repair kit, how much would he spend?

10. If Joey bought a Blitz front light and a Crook Beat padlock and chain, how much would he spend?

Nuts and bolts

Exercise 5

Here is a collection of hexagonal nuts from Joey's bike.
Using a ruler, find out which spanner fits which nut.

Copy the table below and put your answers into it.

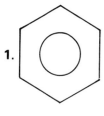 1.
 2.
 3.
 4.
 5.

a.

b.
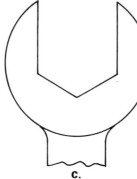
c.

d.

e.

Nut	Spanner	Size
1.	c.	22 mm
2.		
3.		
4.		
5.		

Exercise 6

Use a ruler to decide which nut
fits which bolt.

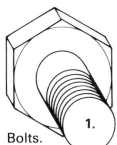
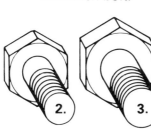
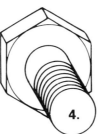
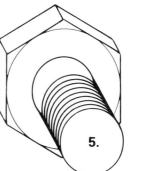

Bolts.

Draw up a table to show your answers.

Nuts.

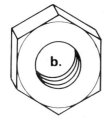

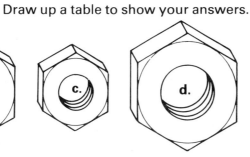
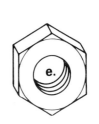
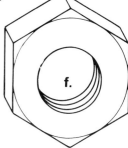

The distance between each marker on the map below is 10 kilometres.
The distance from Joey's home to marker B is 20 kilometres.

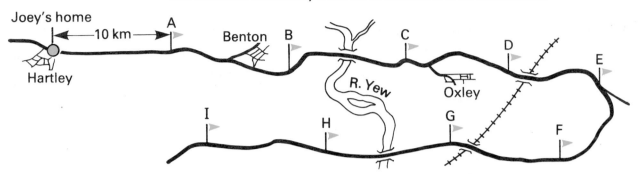

Exercise 7

1. Copy and complete these sentences.

   a. The distance from Joey's home to marker C is _____ kilometres.

   b. The distance from Joey's home to marker F is _____ kilometres.

   c. The distance from Joey's home to marker I is _____ kilometres.

   d. The distance from Joey's home to marker E is _____ kilometres.

2. Joey cycles 10 kilometres in one hour. How many hours will it take to cycle

   a. from home to marker A?   b. from home to marker B?
   c. from home to marker D?   d. from home to marker F?
   e. from home to marker H?   f. from home to marker G?

Exercise 8

Answer the questions below for each of these three speedometers.

a.    b.   c.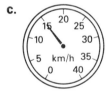

1. What speed is shown on Joey's speedometer?

2. How long would it take him to cycle 30 kilometres at this speed?

3. How long would it take him to cycle 60 kilometres at this speed?

4. If Joey left his home and cycled at this speed for 3 hours, which marker would he reach on the map above?

Exercise 9

If Joey cycles at 20 kilometres per hour, what distance would he cover in these times?

1. 1 hour   2. 2 hours   3. 4 hours   4. $\frac{1}{2}$ hour

5. $1\frac{1}{2}$ hours   6. $3\frac{1}{2}$ hours   7. 6 hours   8. $2\frac{1}{2}$ hours

9. $5\frac{1}{2}$ hours   10. $\frac{1}{4}$ hour   11. $3\frac{1}{4}$ hours   12. $\frac{3}{4}$ hour

On the open road

Exercise 10

Here is a map showing part of Joey's journey.

During the journey he sees a number of road signs. Say where he sees each sign by matching the number on the map with a sign.

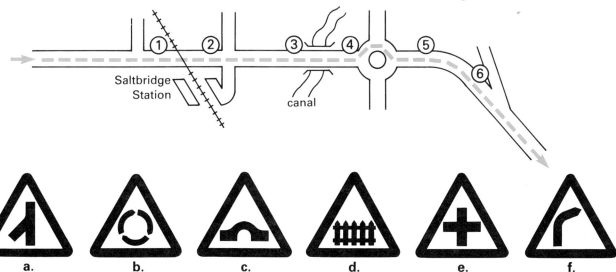

a.   b.   c.   d.   e.   f.

Exercise 11

Here is a map of Joey's journey.

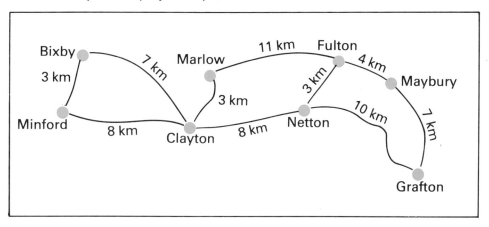

1. Joey starts at Minford, and cycles to Clayton and on to Netton. How far does he travel?

2. From Netton he cycled to Fulton, Maybury and Grafton. How far did he travel?

3. He then cycled to Bixby. How many kilometres is the shortest route?

4. How far is the shortest route between Minford and Fulton?

5. How far is the shortest route between Maybury and Clayton?

6. How far is the shortest route between Marlow and Grafton?

Cycling competition

It is Saturday and Joey is taking part in a cycling competition.

All competitors are timed over three laps of the course.
The quickest time over three laps wins.

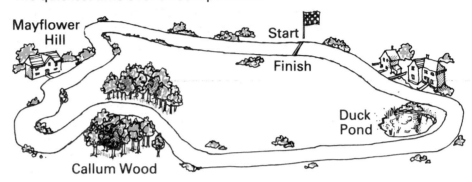

Add up the times of these competitors and answer the questions below.

Toby Carson 19		
	Minutes	Seconds
Lap 1	1	. 20
Lap 2	2	. 12
Lap 3	2	. 26

Ruth Maddocks 27		
	Minutes	Seconds
Lap 1	1	. 30
Lap 2	2	. 05
Lap 3	2	. 18

Joey Greg 31		
	Minutes	Seconds
Lap 1	1	. 32
Lap 2	2	. 09
Lap 3	2	. 10

Mike Hill 22		
	Minutes	Seconds
Lap 1	1	. 18
Lap 2	2	. 35
Lap 3	2	. 41

Remember: 60 seconds equal 1 minute.

Exercise 12

1. Who did the fastest first lap?

2. Who did the fastest second lap?

3. Who did the fastest last lap?

4. How long did Joey take to do the three laps?

5. How long did Ruth take to do the three laps?

6. How long did Toby take to do the three laps?

7. How long did Mike take to do the three laps?

8. Who came first, second, third and fourth?

9. Who took 2 minutes and 5 seconds to complete the second lap?

10. How long did the slowest lap take?

Puzzlers

The Incredible 'Guess Your Age' Machine.

There are five screens on the machine.
On each screen is a group of numbers from 1 to 30.
Look for the screen or screens where your age appears.
When you have found the screen or screens that display your age, count up all the stars above those screens. The number of stars will be equal to your age.

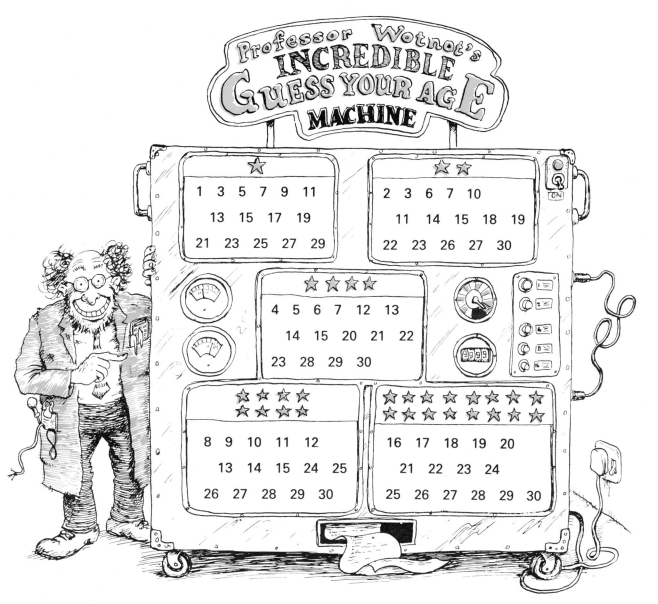

Try it again. See if the machine can guess your shoe size, your favourite number between 1 and 30, or the number of people in your class.

Puzzlers

The Case of the Missing 2p

Tony, Bob, Ann and Jenny are out walking. They decide to buy some sweets.

Bob, Ann and Jenny each have 10p, but Tony has no money.

The three of them agree that if Tony goes to get the sweets, they will give him some.

Tony goes to the shop and spends 26p on Chew Drops. He gets 4p change and runs back to his friends.

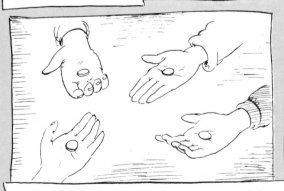

When he returns with the sweets and the 4p change, he gives each of his friends back one penny and they tell him to keep one penny for himself . . . but

Tony gave his friends one penny each, which meant they each paid 9p.

9p + 9p + 9p = 27p

Tony has 1p, which makes 28p.

Since he started with 30p, where is the other 2p?